MW00743461

FOREWORD

Perhaps, as a psychologist and university professor, one of my greatest gifts is discovering that my former students are doing well. Maybe even a greater gift is to discover that my former students are doing good.

Diane Mote is one of my former students. She has a wonderful reputation for being a good therapist, counselor, and parent educator. Now Diane has published this little gem of a book.

Like the very best of therapists, counselors, and parent educators, Diane has learned from her clients. She has done well and she continues to do good.

Read these vignettes and you will be touched, but more important you can learn a lot from her clients. This little book will help you do well and do good.

J. Jeffries McWhirter, Ph.D., ABPP
Professor Emeritus
Counseling and Counseling Psychology Programs
Division of Psychology in Education
Arizona State University

Life can only be understood backwards; it has to be lived forwards.

—Soren Kierkegaard

Text copyright ©2007 by Diane Mote

Cover Design: Debbie Huntsman copyright ©2007

Cover Photography: Karen Walsh Photography copyright ©2007

All rights reserved. Published by AppleStar Publishing LLC, Phoenix

No part of this publication may be reproduced, stored in a retrieval system, or transmitted in any form or by any means, electronic, mechanical, photocopying, recording, or otherwise, without written permission.

Printed in the USA
ISBN-10: 0-9786114-2-X
ISBN-13: 978-0-9786114-2-2

Walking in Backwards

*Vignettes
of Healing
Through Therapy*

DIANE MOTE

For my daughters,
Sara and Amy

*T*his is a collection of vignettes describing therapy sessions with a number of my clients, both children and adults, coping with a wide variety of emotional issues.

Some clients I saw for several years, others for only a few months. Each was memorable in one way or another and represents a universal story or a lesson from the heart.

All clients' names and identifying information have been changed to create composites and to preserve privacy and confidentiality.

My interchange with clients was like nothing I could have anticipated. Together in my consulting room, I often felt we were adrift at sea as the real world faded from view. Our interaction brought an ebb and flow of emotions that at times reached an overwhelming intensity. In the confines of the therapy hour, waves of feeling surged forth in the form of experiences, memories, dreams and fantasies. Rising to the crest has been our liberation.

Table of Contents

Give a man a fish and you feed him for one day. Teach a man to fish and you feed him for a lifetime.

—Chinese proverb

1

Walking in
Backwards

*Four-Year-Old
Anger Management*

Cameron had just turned four years old and was coming for his first session on anger management. Cameron's temper tantrums caused his parents to be at their wits' end. His father in particular was distressed by his inability to control his son. No amount of punishment could thwart a tantrum once Cameron blew.

I told his mother to tell him that he was going to visit a person called a counselor to talk about his angry feelings. I asked her to explain to him that I saw children alone while their mom or dad waited nearby for them, that I had a play room and a treasure box.

When Cameron arrived for his first appointment, I watched him enter down the long brick pathway, walking backwards, with his white "blankie" over his head. Once inside, he let go of his mother's hand and sat gingerly on my couch, still under the blanket. As I tried to draw him out, I had to sit close on the ottoman, leaning over, trying to hear a response if I was lucky enough to get one.

After my introduction and description of my play room, I asked if he had been feeling mad about anything. He answered me with a low growl. I asked him to think about what made him maddest and tell me what that might be. I got more growling at a slightly higher volume. I asked if he was mad at his family, and I got prolonged growling. Finally I said, "Are these questions making you angry?" and that was met with absolute silence. As he sat motionless like a small white mountain, the blanket moved ever so slightly with his breath. We were at a standoff.

The white mound in front of me suddenly made me think of my dog. "Would you like to meet my big white snow dog with blue eyes?"

Cameron swept the blanket off his head and jumped off the couch. "I want to see the snow dog and I saw the movie," he shouted. We were on a roll now.

The blanket stayed crumpled in the corner of the couch as Cameron brushed Isis' thick white coat. I talked about Isis learning good behavior, not having peeing accidents indoors, not chewing pillows, and sleeping in her own bed. He agreed that yelling, hitting and locking her in the kennel wouldn't teach her good behavior. She would just be "more mad and sad." What would work? After some coaching he said, "Treats, reminders, and 'good pats' on the back."

I showed him the scars on her ears that I found when I adopted her from the Pound. "Someone hurt her on both ears, and her dog hair will never grow back in those little places," I told him. "That's really a bad thing to do," he commented as he planted a kiss on each of her scars.

Cameron walked backwards to every session, but he never wore the blankie again or even brought it with him. He also never understood that my dog's name was Isis, and instead called her "Icy." Cameron always wanted to see and talk about "Icy," and we went over the same stories of her misbehavior and how to fix it. He inspected her ears each time, as if he expected them to heal. Right along with Isis' maturation, Cameron's behavior improved, and I continued to thank him for all his help with "Icy."

Winning over Cameron was one of the first times I had used my dog in a therapy session. That day proved pivotal: I had a captivating therapy tool practically within my arm's reach. With Cameron and countless other children, Isis has facilitated growth, change, understanding and self-esteem.

"I's a mad boy alls the time," Cameron initially confided with a deep sigh.

"How do you show your mad feelings?" I questioned.

"I's hit, kick, scratch, and scream until my mommy puts me away," he confessed.

"Do you bite?" I inquired.

No, he didn't do that anymore, he explained, shaking his head for emphasis. I congratulated him on learning not to bite and suggested if he could control that, he could learn some other ways to express his anger.

I believed Cameron needed to effect change in something else before he could believe it was possible for him to change. He needed to show kindness toward something more helpless than himself in order to view himself as a kind and good little boy.

We set to work on training Isis. I made a list of all of Isis' transgressions, from accidental peeing, destructive chewing, and even whining. I asked Cameron for help with teaching her some new behaviors. First, I wanted him to tell me what would not help her be a kind and good dog. I wrote down all of his thoughts which, over the course of a few months, became prolific.

Among those which clearly represented his own fears were: don't say "you's a bad dog," "take her toys away," "leave her all alone" or "forget to pet her." There were also admonitions against using a mean voice, smacking, hitting with a newspaper, or putting her to bed without dinner. I also asked Cameron what to do with my own feelings of frustration when Isis would chew one of my couch pillows or knock over her water bowl. With the authority only a four year old could muster he blurted out, "Say to yourself she's just a dog," in effect counseling me that I might need to change some of my own expectations and my perspective on dog behaviors.

At each session, Cameron wanted to know how Isis' week had been. He relished any stories of naughty behavior. As affirming as it might be that both dogs and young children can be disobedient, he never suggested we punish her. He would pat her, say he had some troubles too, and give her what I coined a "pup talk."

I urged Cameron's parents to have discussions with him about his misbehavior only when each of them was calm and able to think clearly. This problem-solving discussion would include asking Cameron what a better choice might have been. I asked them to encourage Cameron to use other strategies to express his anger. One of the most successful was making angry pictures using different colors for each feeling he was experiencing at the time. Sometimes he gave the picture a title.

Cameron brought a scrapbook of his "feelings" pictures for me to look at during one of our sessions and seemed particularly proud of his "book of mad and sad days." His favorite drawing he labeled "Hurricane" because he had cried so much that day when he was sent for a timeout after pushing his little sister.

He continued to assure me the "pup talks" were helping him at home and that he thought both he and Icy were doing better. I decided Cameron's mispronunciation was therapeutic serendipity and did not correct him.

Life does not consist mainly or even largely of facts and happenings. It consists mainly of the storm of thoughts that are forever blowing through one's mind.

—Mark Twain

2

Floating
Fear

Panic Attacks

There was a recurring dream Marcie had as a child that lasted through many years. She never revealed it to anyone and doesn't remember even considering "telling." As a child she thought she had to live with it. As an adult, Marcie realized she could neither confide in her father for fear of ridicule, nor in her mother for fear of rejection.

As the dream began, Marcie was alone in her house, and she saw a man peering through the window. Immediately, she felt threatened and terrified. She drew the draperies closed as her breathing quickened. As she covered each window she saw his monstrous-looking face, determined to get in. Running from room to room, she drew the curtains over that face. Then she saw the knob of the front door turning, and she pushed against the door with all her might, her small frame no match for him. She always awoke at the same point in the dream—just when his strong, hairy hand grabbed her and began to pull her through the doorway.

Marcie's fear of the dark was profound and secret. Many nights she lay frozen until sleep came, too frightened to move, cry out or confide in anyone. It was during these times that the "spiders" began to haunt her. As she remembered it now, she lay awake and desperately tried not to think of "spiders." To think of them was to call them to her. With eyes wide open, Marcie involuntarily summoned the red dots and dashes that were her "spiders" into the darkness of her room. They were not scary to look at in and of themselves; but the idea of bringing something from her imagination into the concrete reality of her bedroom terrified her. She watched the spiders until, exhausted, she fell asleep.

Another recurring event in Marcie's life also seemed, in hindsight, to be a hallucination. When she was in junior high school, she recalled the repeated sensation that she was being stalked as she walked to meet her boyfriend. They each had about a mile to walk to a place halfway between their houses. Marcie remembered single men in cars driving slowly next to her, following her. She would break into a sprint and run through people's front yards to stay away from the street. Only when her boyfriend was in sight would she dare to look at the street, but by then there would be no car in sight.

Marcie never forgot about the dream of the hand, the hallucination of "spiders," or the men in cars stalking her, but the fears stopped as unexpectedly as they had come. As an adult, she wondered if she had been on the verge of a psychotic break when left alone to face her fears.

Marcie had no memory of physical affection from her mother. She thought it must have existed during her infancy or as a toddler, but she had no memories or photos to confirm it. Mostly, she recalled her own stoicism and the secret fears of her youth. Fear of the dark, kidnappers, scorpions, black widows, drowning and dying had occupied her thoughts daily. Marcie kept her fears to herself until she came to see me about her panic attacks. She had begun to experience frequent panic, without reason, not when she saw a spider or saw an accident, but simply "out of the blue."

She could be driving her children to school, shopping, or having lunch with a friend when fear would grab her. Physically she felt as if she might die or completely lose control of herself. Marcie had recently bolted from the grocery store, leaving behind a cart full of food, because she had been too stricken to write a check. Her mind had stopped functioning, and her hand had cramped. She was momentarily frozen.

One of Marcie's panic attacks occurred while she was on her way to my office. Her palms were sweating as she alternately wiped her hands on her pants, swept the tears from her face, and replaced her hands on the steering wheel. Fear had consumed her to the point where she could hold only one thought as she drove to her session with me: "Save me."

She was running up my steps when I opened the door to a visibly frightened young woman. Marcie was hyperventilating, crying and shaking uncontrollably as I led her to the sofa.

"I can't breathe," she said through gasps for air.

"You're having a panic attack, but it won't kill you. Try to slow down your breathing."

Her hands were cramping, I explained, due to the decrease in blood flow to her extremities.

"No one has ever died from one of these?" she asked.

"Not that I know of," I reassured her, "and you won't be the first."

After she had done some deep breathing

and drank a few sips of water, I asked Marcie to recognize how much calmer she had become in just a matter of a few minutes.

Slowly we began an exploration of Marcie's fearful memories. Many children are haunted by their fears, but Marcie's childhood had been dominated by them. Black widows didn't roam the house, but they formed intricate webs outside. After dark, Marcie and her brothers hunted the spiders with flashlights blazing and a can of insecticide. She recalled the time one of her brothers walked into a web, and the black widow scrambled up his shirt while the other brother drenched it in spray. It fell to the ground, instantly immobilized, with its orange hourglass illuminated in the moonlight.

Then there were the strangers: in the middle of the night a man was found kneeling next to the bed of a young girl in her neighborhood. There was the man who pulled up in a car next to Marcie and exposed himself when she was walking on the sidewalk to a friend's house. She was even taken to the police station to view a lineup. There was the substitute teacher at her school who took her and her friends into the closet, one by one. Marcie had said "no" to his advances, and he had let her go after she promised not to tell.

Also during her childhood, Marcie saw several drowning victims. One was an elderly neighbor who had gone swimming alone. She saw his body in the pool, blue and contorted by rigor mortis, through a hole in the fence. Another drowning was of a baby in a play pool. Marcie had sometimes been a babysitter for the child. Then there was the adolescent drowning victim who survived, but lived permanently thereafter in a wheelchair, unable to communicate. His family brought him to all the neighborhood block parties and attended to him as though nothing was wrong. People even threw him a beach ball despite knowing he couldn't return it.

Marcie experienced all of these tragic events alone, protected only by her own sheer will and without the support of a family to offer her a sense of security.

Had she been on the brink of a psychotic break? Probably not, as there was always a basis in reality for her fear. Perhaps she experienced the world differently because of her heightened sensitivity and vivid imagination which fueled her fears.

With medication to calm her panic disorder and with the support, reassurance and guidance of therapy, Marcie learned to confront and control her fears. As an adult she was finally able to escape the demons which had haunted her as a child.

Madness is the result not of uncertainty but certainty.

—Friedrich Nietzsche

3

Rituals

OCD Compulsions

Lawrence sat inside his car for eleven minutes before entering my office. He timed it on his watch and waited for the "magic" number to release him. His physician had suggested he see someone to help him deal with his obsessive compulsive disorder (OCD) because checking, counting and cleaning consumed a large part of each of his days. He was very nervous during our early sessions, clearing his throat often, picking lint off the armrest and having trouble making eye contact. He was well dressed and nice looking, but he had an unnatural "no hair out of place" presence. When describing his rituals, he would sometimes laugh self-consciously or slowly shake his head, seemingly mystified by his own behavior. "I buy Clorox towelettes by the case and use at least one canister a day," he confessed.

Leaving his house was a struggle. He felt safe sitting or driving in his car, but not getting out to enter new or even familiar places. Dry cleaning, groceries, and videos were all delivered to him, so his contact with other people was minimal. He worked at home in a moderately successful online business, and he emerged from his house only twice a day, for two reasons.

The easier task was to retrieve the mail. This ordeal took several minutes and involved several hand washings, counting and depositing the mail in a plastic bag to bring inside. Each piece of mail was then sprayed with disinfectant and either thrown away immediately or opened, read and filed.

The other task for which Lawrence left the house was more ominous and involved emptying the garbage and sorting objects for recycling. This took several more minutes of hand washing and packaging and was always performed precisely at 11 a.m.

During our first visit, Lawrence told me his psychiatrist wanted him to tame the "wild beast" that was his OCD and had started him on medication. I told him that the "wild beast" was actually a helpful metaphor because I believed he could begin to learn to control his symptoms instead of letting his symptoms control him.

In one of our sessions, Lawrence brought up his earliest traumatic memory, which was of the day his grandfather had a heart attack while sitting on the porch swing. Grandpa Jim had been watching Lawrence ride his bike when he suddenly and simply fell forward. The emergency vehicles came, and Grandpa Jim was pronounced dead on arrival. Lawrence had been the only witness to his grandfather's death.

Everyone wanted to know what Grandpa Jim had said to Lawrence before he died, and when exactly (or whether) Lawrence had seen him fall. Lawrence didn't know the answers to these questions, then or now. He hadn't really been paying that much attention to Grandpa Jim, but he didn't know how he could tell anyone that.

"Do you think a child should feel guilty about his grandfather having a heart attack while they were together?" I asked.

Lawrence shook his head in that mystified way of his and said, "No, but I do feel that I might have done something wrong."

No matter how much reassurance he was offered by his family and others, Lawrence had passed his own sentence of guilt on himself. The counting, checking and cleaning had begun in earnest the year his grandfather died when Lawrence was ten years old. Time seemed only to worsen his symptoms, not to alleviate them.

"What if you just stopped the rituals? What would the result be?" I pressed.

He wasn't sure; he just knew it would be something bad—his death, someone else's death, perhaps?

"Like Grandpa Jim's," I offered.

"Yes, I suppose so. I know logically that's not true, that it wasn't my fault, but I still feel as if it was."

A child's natural egocentricism often leads to a false sense of responsibility for an event that might be witnessed, but not caused by his actions or inactions. The well-meaning questions of his family had only compounded the problem for Lawrence, making him feel that his negligence, in some way, had contributed to his grandfather's death.

When I began seeing Lawrence, he was a young bachelor with a long history of OCD, which had become worse since he graduated from college and had begun living alone. As he became more reclusive, he spent increasing amounts of time performing his rituals. As Lawrence and I moved forward, I hoped he would learn to manage the behaviors associated with his OCD, and that his own strength would render the beast powerless.

We came up with a behavior modification program to monitor and disrupt his dysfunctional habits, and he began making some progress. Lawrence never missed an appointment until I got a voice mail that he was ill and running a fever.

I returned the call and urged him to see a doctor if the fever did not break. Two days later Lawrence called from his hospital bed to tell me he had called 911 the night before because his fever peaked at 104 degrees, and he became too weak to get himself to the hospital. He had managed to pack an overnight bag despite his worsening symptoms, and although he packed four canisters of Clorox towelettes, they remained unopened and unused at the hospital. He was diagnosed with pneumonia and seemed quite despondent about his recovery.

I knew he was facing some of his worst fears, so I offered to visit him. Our conversation was mostly about something I had said a few sessions earlier. I commented that perhaps he was doing his immune system a disservice by limiting his exposure to people, the environment and even the germs in his own apartment. He conceded that I was probably right, and that he might now be dying. I reassured him that he was not on a critical care unit, and that he should ask his nurse about his prognosis. His nurse was all smiles when she told him it would be only a matter of days until he was on his way home.

The Clorox towelettes remained untouched the entire time he was at the hospital. Lawrence just hadn't the strength to get up and clean anything. Nothing in the hospital was under his control. He tried counting, but there was no rhyme or reason to it. It was not at all like it was at home where counting, checking and cleaning controlled everything. He was not in control anymore, and he was forced to recognize that the certainty he thought his rituals provided was an illusion.

The next time I saw Lawrence, he seemed cured or nearly cured of the debilitating effects of his OCD. Freud described what he called a "flight into health," which could occur for various reasons, but sometimes seemingly out of the blue. When Lawrence returned home, he felt he had been released by the recognition that all of the "protection" he felt was provided by his rituals had actually backfired, and that he no longer felt compelled to perform them. He rejoiced to me that he was "not dead," was "feeling a whole lot better" and even described himself as "lighthearted."

Lawrence stayed committed to his behavior modification program. He laughed more. He told me he stopped "freaking out" and could now be described at worst as only a "neatnik." He became what Freud called the "healthy neurotic" and now exhibited no more than the idiosyncrasies that most of us display. Last year, he attended his fifth college reunion, carrying only one canister of towelettes in his suitcase.

Play therapy has become the main avenue for helping young children with their emotional difficulties.

—Bruno Bettelheim

4

Red Light

*Kindergarten
Discipline*

If Joey got off the school bus holding one hand behind his back and hanging his head, this was a signal to his mother that he'd had another day of failure. He was only in kindergarten, but already there was talk among the school officials of retention, special education and a clinical diagnosis.

The first time Joey came to see me, he had his hand hidden behind his back. "I guess there is something you are hiding from me," I ventured. "Would you like to find something to play with on my toy shelf or show me your hand first?"

He brought his hand forward slowly and said almost inaudibly, "I got a red light today." On the back of his hand was drawn a well-proportioned traffic signal, with a red stop light colored in. The smudges told me there had been some effort toward erasing it.

I was familiar with the behavior modification program used at Joey's school, but curious how he would explain it. "Tell me about that stop light. What does it mean?" I asked.

He told me it was "a very bad thing," even a yellow light meant "you weren't good," "only a green light is good." "You did everything right if you had a green light that day."

I asked who would draw the light on his hand, and he said his teacher would at the end of each school day. He wouldn't peek while she was making the traffic sign on his hand because he was afraid to see which light she would be giving him.

"Is it hard to watch because you wish it would be a green light?" I suggested.

He sighed and said, "I thinked maybe if she gave me more chances and it won't be a red light."

I asked how many chances did he think he needed, and his answer reflected how disheartened he was. "Infinity." I asked him to describe infinity, and he said "Numbers that don't stop, they just keep going." With arms waving in big circles, he boasted, "I learned that in my school."

I asked Joey what the highest number he could think of would be, and he replied, "A zillion." I agreed that was probably my highest number, too.

I asked why his teacher hadn't written the traffic lights on paper, and he replied promptly, "I losed all the red light papers. My mom is supposed to sign the paper and put it in my backpack. My teacher said I can't lose my hand." His nervous laughter made it clear he understood both the joke and the reprimand.

Joey was a chip off the old block, and I found his father John's behavior far more challenging to address than his son's. John wanted a quick fix to his son's behavioral issues and checked his wrist watch several times during our sessions. John was a pilot, and he was certain there was a way he could control his five-year-old child. After all, he controlled transatlantic jets in the sky.

During our first therapy session, he asked me for one behavioral technique he could use all the time with Joey and for any misbehavior. I told him I knew of many strategies and techniques to modify a child's behavior, but child rearing was not a one-size-fits-all proposition. John shook his head and looked irritated, exhibiting a body language that said I was making this far more complicated than it needed to be.

John didn't particularly like spanking Joey, but it was his tool of choice in disciplining his son. He couldn't grasp why his son did not respond to his threats; Joey knew full well if he brought a red light home he would get a spanking from Dad right after dinner. On those evenings, Joey ate well, played with his sister and acted as though no whipping awaited him behind the bedroom door. John told me how Joey would lie on his bed, make his body rigid and cover his eyes with his hands, burying his head in his pillow. John would give him a few hard smacks and tell him he'd better straighten up, then stomp out of the room while his son cried to himself.

Once John had even used his belt as he railed against his son, reminiscent of his own father. The belt left bruises on Joey's legs and buttocks. Joey held nothing against his dad and told me his dad spanked him to get out the "bad stuff," but it just hadn't worked yet. He loved his dad and believed his dad loved him.

I asked Joey if when he grew up and was a dad if he would spank his own son. He told me he didn't know, that he just might have no kids, but some pets. When I pointed out that sometimes people hit animals to get them to behave, he said that was mean and you could just send them outside. After several minutes of silence while he was building a skate board park with blocks and ramps, he looked at me and said, "My mom says I can't hit my sister when she does something wrong, so I wish she'd tell my dad not to hit me when I do something wrong. She said my sister is little and doesn't know a lot and I need to teach her stuff. Maybe my dad thinks I can't learn."

I assured Joey I would help his father teach him some new behaviors instead of punishing him with spankings and that he seemed to be learning that very moment to think things through and make better choices.

We played school in my consulting room for many months. I was the recalcitrant student and he was the teacher. He gave me red lights, yellow lights and green lights with a surprisingly mature sense of justice, sometimes holding fast to protocol, other times generously giving me a "taste of infinity."

We designed a book of traffic signals that was tied to his backpack so he would have a weekly record of his progress at school. I "reframed" (a technique therapists often use to help a client see a different perspective) the meaning of the traffic signals: green lights stood for "going forward" days, yellow lights represented "slowing down and needing to use caution" days, and red lights signaled "stop to think and learn from your behavior" days.

I told him that, like drivers on the road, we learn to control ourselves by stopping at the red light, even when we are in a hurry. It was a rule (law) we could take with us, wherever we found ourselves. There were imaginary red lights almost everywhere: at school, in our neighborhood, in the park, and in our own homes. The traffic light could also be imagined as a voice inside us, sometimes quiet and sometimes loud that might say, "go ahead," "be careful," or "stop, make a different choice in your behavior."

Joey continued to receive some red lights, but they became few and far between. When he got a yellow light, he perceived it as an almost green light instead of an almost red light. There were no rewards or punishments, just indicators of progress. A green light meant he was growing up and learning the rules, a yellow light that he needed some reminders of appropriate behavior, and a red light was for a mistake in behavior or error in judgment to be discussed with me or his parents.

At my suggestion, Father and son went over Joey's book of traffic signals on a daily basis, with the emphasis on encouragement and no punishments for any red lights. John said it would be a miracle if Joey's behavior changed without consequences for misbehavior and no rewards, either. I told him his own fatherly concern and attention were all Joey needed and to be patient. Sure enough, one day I received a voice mail from John confirming that Joey was on a new path and that maybe I had been right; all his son had really needed was a dose of encouragement and understanding.

The clincher came when Joey rushed into a session waving a piece of paper and shouting, "Just like me, just like me! Daddy got a red light just like me!" And indeed, his father had received a traffic ticket for going through a red light and had been man enough to show it to his son so they could both be comrades in arms.

Never turn your back on tears.

Do not stem the flow.

Knowing why is not important; weeping sometimes is.

—Ruth Bell Graham

5

Puppy Love

Loss of a Childhood

What Nora remembered most clearly was the Romeo and Juliet quality of their relationship. She was 12 and Cody was 13 when they met, and for a few years they were inseparable. Nora explained that her love for Cody then rivaled that which she had later given to men in her adult life, in the depth of its caring and devotion. I agreed that there was an undeniable intensity that youth could bring to love which defied the stereotype of "puppy love." However, the foundation of their connection was one of desperation, rather than maturity. Cody had a father who beat him regularly with a belt, a mother who drank and a brother who had trouble with the law. Nora was a street kid, smart, sassy and adventurous. Her father was unknown, and her mother had a string of affairs with less than desirable men.

Nora and Cody's young relationship was rooted in the unmet need for nurturing from their respective parents, which they were able to find in each other's tenderness. They hadn't known each other much longer than six months when there was a turning point to a deeper and more profound relationship.

Cody's parents had invited Nora to visit their cabin in the pines for a weekend retreat. The two of them slept on cots in sleeping bags a few feet apart.

That night his parents had a violent argument, which left Nora shaking as she listened to the banging of pots and pans while curse words flew back and forth. She looked over at Cody's sleeping bag but couldn't distinguish his face. Instinctively, she reached over to Cody in the dark. He took her hand and wrapped both hands around it. His body was trembling, and she knew he was sobbing. She felt the urge to both pull away and put her arms around him. Nora left her hand in his, moved by his need for comfort and trust in her.

When the voices of his parents died down, they slept motionless until she was suddenly awakened when he climbed into the sleeping bag next to her. They wrapped their arms around each other and a bond was formed that night. There was no sex, only the desire to be held, understood and cherished, born of the parental neglect which they saw mirrored in each other.

Did I believe love between two adolescents could be the real thing? Nora wanted answers, but I had learned that clients don't really want the therapist to answer their questions. They just think they do. They suppose an answer can be a way out of their pain or can bring a final resolution to a dilemma, but experience teaches otherwise. What Nora really needed was to explore her uncertainty and come to terms with her own answers about love.

I asked her to tell me more about Cody and why the camping memory was such a strong one. "It was the beginning of a great romance," she said. "He gave me a silver ring with a horse's head carved on it. Our favorite game was to play hide-and-seek in the orange grove near his house." The "seeker" would look for clues of arrows made with rocks or fallen oranges arranged as arrow shapes.

One day Cody constructed a huge heart out of about fifty oranges on the ground. When Nora found it, Cody jumped out of a tree in front of her and said, "I'm a Boy Scout and this is my pledge to you." He proudly presented the heart of oranges with a sweep of his arm.

He made "butt seats" on the bank of one of the irrigation ditches in the grove, so they could have permanent "chairs" under the shady branches of an orange tree. After irrigation, the dirt was damp, and it would cool your entire body if you sat there for awhile. Cody had "drink holders" scooped out beside the seats so they could sip colas while they planned their future.

One day as they sat by the ditch, the irrigation water came roaring toward them like a pipeline. They climbed into a tree and watched the grove fill up with water. Cody was the first to start laughing at their predicament. He told Nora to climb from the tree onto his back. He piggybacked her over and across the rows of ditches to dry land. "We were the same size then, that age where boys haven't hit a growth spurt yet, but most of the girls are developing and have grown taller. He was puffing from going up and down those little hills. Do you know he never even swore at me, when we got into an argument?" They planned to get married when they became of legal age and rejected the idea of needing more life experience under their belts.

With high school, however, everything changed. Cody began hanging out with a group of "rough kids," and when Nora was 15 she decided to break up with him. The reasons were summed up in one word: "delinquent" behavior, which he refused to change even though she had given him many ultimatums which he had chosen to ignore. He was still drinking beer, carrying a pocket knife and running away from home.

Just two months after the break up, tragedy struck. Cody died in a rollover accident on the highway, just weeks after his 16th birthday. Nora became reclusive and lonely, let her grades plummet and felt only an empty aching inside when she remembered Cody.

Her year of therapy with me began when she was still a teenager, suggested by her family physician, right before she left for college. In one of our last sessions, Nora answered some of her own questions. It was as though the understanding had been inside her all the time; she just hadn't uncovered it. She asked me if I had heard of the quote, "It is better to have loved and lost, than never to have loved at all." She said she embraced that thought because it validated her pain and guilt over Cody. "I was just so young when I thought I had lost my chance at love," Nora said, "that I didn't know how to understand or define it. We were just two kids running from a painful childhood, and for awhile we were winning the race."

5 Puppy Love

What lies behind us, and what lies before us are tiny matters, compared to what lies within us.

—Ralph Waldo Emerson

6

Awaiting Grace

A Childhood Trauma

At Celeste's first session she confided, "I'm confused about some memories I have about my mother and me. I don't know if what I remember is what actually happened or not. There is one memory that especially bothers me, or I should say pieces of a memory."

I suggested that memories often were not cohesive. Possibly we could connect her fragmented thoughts to her feelings surrounding the memory.

"It was such a long time ago." Her voice trailed off as she wiped tears from her eyes.

We talked about the past and one's perception of the past, how separate realities could co-exist for different people, each could be valid and real. An objective, shared reality might not exist. I told Celeste I thought her recollections could offer a new clarity about her past because, as adults, we could explore mature interpretations of her experiences. We may never know the absolute truth reflected in her early memories, but we would know the truth of her feelings and fears as she put them together in our sessions.

I asked her to start with the experience that most confused and troubled her. She was seven years old in the first grade and idolized her classroom teacher. One of the special privileges that Miss Andrews offered was staying in for lunch recess and helping to decorate the bulletin boards. Celeste was delighted when she was chosen to be the special helper.

While helping, Celeste stood on a folding chair to reach the bulletin board. Miss Andrews was singing and had her back turned, shuffling some papers on her desk when the folding chair suddenly collapsed beneath Celeste. She had been standing on the tips of her toes in an effort to reach way up high when the chair abruptly folded. Because she had fallen with one leg on each side of the chair, the top of the chair slammed into her crotch.

Celeste was dazed, hurt, scared and thought she'd wet her pants. It was Miss Andrews who noticed while helping her up that blood was streaming down her legs. "My teacher carried me all the way to the nurse's office, one arm under my knees and the other arm under my head," Celeste recalled. "I wanted Miss Andrews to stay with me, but she told me she couldn't, and I think the nurse had to pry me away from her. Then the nurse wanted me to take off my blood soaked underwear."

She remembered running to the corner of the nurse's office and sitting on the floor with her arms around her knees shouting, "I won't, I won't do that." Celeste was still in that corner when her mother came to pick her up, and they drove straight to their family pediatrician. She had no memory of what happened at the doctor's office.

I explained that sometimes we forget traumatic events as a way of protecting ourselves, and that our minds act as a shield to fear. I told her I thought she could assume everything was handled appropriately, in spite of her anxiety both then and now.

I asked Celeste what was most vivid about her memory of the accident, and her immediate thought was of the cleansings which were repeated daily by her mother. "My mother did them on the floor in the bathroom, and I had to lie on newspapers while she washed my vaginal area with some disinfectant from the doctor's. It would burn, and I would try to push her hands away and she would scold me. I suppose it was necessary," Celeste said hesitantly.

"I suppose it was," I interjected, "But I think it was your mother's manner you are questioning."

Celeste decided that was true. She had the critical pieces of her memory: the painful cleansings, lying on the newspapers, and the reprimands when she protested. It was the absence of a caress that she found most disheartening and was brought to the surface in her next associative thought.

It was not the first time that newspapers had been strewn on the bathroom floor. When her dog had puppies, the bathroom was the birthing place, and she had seen the puppies, with eyes still shut, crawling in the afterbirth. Then as a young child, Celeste, like her pet, had lain on newspapers with her own vaginal wound.

There had been episodes of depression in Celeste's life, but she had persevered and not sought psychotherapy. She had been afraid to open up and trust someone other than her husband. At our first session she told me about an article she had read that described psychotherapy as a process like peeling an onion layer by layer. The analogy bothered her as she envisioned the thin layers of her psyche being peeled back, the endless tears, exposing the core of herself. "There is nothing about an onion I can relate to," she told me. "Peeling them makes me cry and eating one doesn't agree with me."

"Let's talk about your concerns in a different way then," I offered. "Are you comfortable talking about whatever comes into your mind?

"It's okay to ramble, to start and stop, to talk about the past and present as if they run together and to just let your thoughts spill forth," I suggested, in an effort to put her at ease.

Celeste's childhood was a mix of episodes of neglect by her parents, interspersed with intercontinental trips and vacations. Most of the time she had been raised by a nanny. When her mother was home, she was seldom interested in parenting her daughter. Celeste had adored her father, and when he would return from abroad it felt like a gift had arrived at her door. He often brought her trinkets from his travels, but always left her yearning for a stronger relationship.

For high school Celeste was sent to boarding school in the East and never returned to live at home again. Boarding school had been lonely, but she had done well, and she had met Adam. They went to college together, with Celeste studying art and Adam studying architecture. Celeste and Adam had married during their senior year of college, six years before I met her.

Celeste was a sculptress and brought me photographs of her work. One was of a baby, a cherub, in a gentle pose, lying on his back, looking to the side.

"How did you do that?" I inquired.

Celeste said she had used her nephew as the model and also studied photographs of babies. "This is the child I want," she said in a trembling voice with her eyes brimming. "My husband and I are taking fertility treatments, which we have kept private, but nothing seems to be working. I'm depressed, and my doctor thinks that my depression is interfering with pregnancy."

Her voice shook as she elaborated on her doctor's concern. Which comes first, is it the chicken or the egg? Was she depressed because she couldn't get pregnant or had her infertility caused her depression? "This is tearing me up inside. I'm asking for your help," Celeste leaned toward me with her palms open.

I asked about her childhood injury with the folding chair and whether she had been permanently damaged, but she assured me her doctors had told her she was physically fine. She spoke of her childhood in a rote fashion except for a few bright memories of her father. She remained confused about her mother and was unable to conjure up a recollection that might speak to a strong connection between them.

One session she related, "I would watch her while she was doing things around the house. I would be sitting and looking at her or standing still in front of her, but she would not see me. Does that sound crazy?"

I thought I knew what she meant and gently explained, "Not at all. It is a classic sign of neglect; not being seen leaves one diminished and starving for love and validation. No wonder you have dealt with depression for much of your life, yet it would have been worse if you had not had the sustenance of other loving relationships." Celeste's father, her nanny, her aunt and a few of her teachers had been instrumental in providing Celeste with the stability she needed to grow into adulthood.

Celeste felt she had much love to give but nothing to focus it on except the hoped-for pregnancy. Adam had suggested that maybe a pet would help in the meantime, directing her thoughts, energy and caresses to an actual living creature. He decided that a labrador retriever, a breed known for its affectionate nature, would do the trick, and Celeste suddenly had her hands and heart full. I encouraged her to contact her parents, tell them of her struggle to become pregnant, and find some level of peace in these relationships.

Her father lived abroad, but he quickly responded with a loving note, including expressed regret for not keeping more in touch. Her mother lived across the country now, having divorced Celeste's father while Celeste was in boarding school. Celeste did not hear from her, but she did write to her favorite aunt, who came to visit and to meet the puppy. She confided more in a few friends who had wrongly assumed that her art was fulfilling her dreams.

Without medication, Celeste's depression slowly seemed to lift, and she came to terms with her infertility, neither blaming herself or her husband. The doctors informed her they just didn't know why there was a problem or if she would ever have a baby.

After a year of therapy, Celeste brought up the subject of adoption, and she and Adam went through the process of registering for a foreign adoption. She said she couldn't imagine greater happiness than having her own baby.

Adam and Celeste waited almost a year for eight-month-old Juan to arrive from Guatemala. He came wrapped in colorful woven blankets, in cloth diapers, with two changes of outfits in a small bag with his name taped to the outside. The nurse who brought him carefully placed him in Celeste's arms, telling her in Spanish to love and keep him.

Juan was three years old when Celeste told him a story about the cherub sculpture that she had molded years before. "The sculpture was my wish for you before you were born. Then one day the news came you were flying to America to find me," she recalled explaining to him. He told the story to all who would listen, embellishing it as he grew older.

His revised version became: "My mamma had a wish for me to be her baby, so she made a sculpture of a baby, and I was born and then I flew to America to find my mamma, forever."

The year Juan turned four, Celeste began to teach him to mold his own sculptures. Her own work was exhibited at a local museum, and she discovered to her surprise that she was pregnant. We reconnected for awhile after she left me a joyful voicemail saying, "After waiting ten years, as soon as I felt her moving inside me, I knew her name would be Grace."

The soul becomes dyed by the color of its thoughts.

—Marcus Aurelius

7

Faith
Healing

*A Search for
Spiritual Peace*

Jane's best friend was Ariel, an only child of divorced parents. Ariel's mother was a bewitching and beguiling person who looked like Marilyn Monroe. She took nude sunbaths in her backyard. Her usual attire was a negligee, and when Jane came to visit she would respond to Jane's knock with "Just come in, dear," and not disturb herself from a yoga position.

Jane knew her as Minister Bordeaux, as she was called by a small group of odd women who met regularly at her home. The meetings started at dusk, and when Jane spent the night with Ariel, they would press their ears against the door of the studio to hear the low chanting voices of her mother's congregation. Looking through the partially separated curtains into the studio, Jane and Ariel witnessed the women holding hands and chanting, their dancing shadows cast by candlelight. Occasionally, one of them would fall to the ground and begin a deep wailing which became intertwined with the constant chanting. Giggles might escape their mouths as they pressed up against the window, but Jane also felt she might cry instead of laugh.

Jane was eight years old when she began to regularly spend weekend nights at Ariel's home. The girls often had the run of the house while Ariel's mother ministered to her guests in the studio. Jane frequently suffered from ear infections that woke her in the middle of the night, from which Minister Bordeaux tried to "heal" her. Jane remembered Bordeaux's hand cupped over her ear, holding Jane's head tilted up as she prayed, and pressing Jane's face against Minister Bordeaux's chest as she held her tight. Jane wanted only to pull away from the softness of her breast, the moistness of her skin and the suffocating embrace.

Jane endured Minister Bordeau's prayers as long as she could, but then complained that her ear was still painful. In obvious frustration, Bordeaux suggested it was Jane's lack of faith that interfered with her healing powers and instructed Jane to call her parents to take her home. As this scenario was repeated, the intensity of Bordeaux's healing rituals increased, and Jane's sense of guilt was magnified. Alarmed by the fire in Minister Bordeaux's eyes, Jane would sometimes whimper "Please, please, let me go home. I want to call my dad."

Minister Bordeaux professed to have had "out of body experiences" and told titillating stories of her adventures. She promised to teach Ariel and Jane the techniques of soul travel. They were cautioned, however, not to think about this idea of soul release on their own or they could inadvertently cause their soul's escape and possible death. Jane was told that once her soul was free, the likelihood of retrieving it was almost nil for an "untrained pilot." Minister Bordeaux said she could save her daughter's soul from a night's wanderings, but she had no such consolation for Jane. Going to sleep at Ariel's became a terror-stricken experience of "thinking about the unthinkable," which made fear loom even larger in her mind.

One night as she lay in bed at Ariel's, panic caused Jane to fake an ear infection. She demanded to call her father. "Your healing doesn't work. I'm sorry, I'm sorry," she pleaded. In the car with her father, she confided all the fearful stories that Minister Bordeaux had so elaborately strung together. Her father began to laugh as he reached over to pull Ariel closer to him. He wasn't irritated that she had gotten him up in the middle of the night, or that she had lied to get him to come pick her up. "She's a fruitcake," he said calmly, and the terror in her tender soul was put to rest in his embrace.

This was one of Jane's earliest memories of a spiritual dilemma that would haunt her for many years. Minister Bordeaux was her friend's mother, at times doting and generous, but when she heard "the word of God," she became driven and controlling. Her eyes took on a glazed look, her jaw tensed, and she moved in long strides with her filmy nightclothes swaying in the breeze. She claimed her daughter never got sick because she was "saved" and under her mother's healing umbrella. Jane wanted that too, but wishful thinking and even praying didn't seem to make a difference. Although she took solace in her father's dismissal of Minister Bordeaux, Jane was never sure he was absolutely right. The conviction Minister Bordeaux demonstrated was mesmerizing.

As Jane became more and more uncomfortable with Ariel's mother and her bizarre behavior, their friendship began to fall apart. Jane refused to spend the night because of her fears of illness, botched healing and "soul travel." She found a book on soul travel in the witchcraft section of a used bookstore and developed a profound fear of the occult. After seeing the movie, *Rosemary's Baby*, Jane became so fearful of the dark that she slept with the light on and six crosses of various sizes lined up on her bureau.

During high school Jane went on a spiritual quest exploring different religions, including attending a Billy Graham revival. A young man next to her fell to the ground in a spasm and began "talking in tongues." People around her were exclaiming "Praise the Lord" with their arms raised and swaying from side to side. Later, she saw the boy's mother write a check to the Billy Graham crusade, and one of the attendants gave the boy a Milky Way bar. Jane wondered why God hadn't chosen her for a special purpose—to be a minister who looked like Marilyn Monroe, to be a soul traveler, or to "talk in tongues" and be "saved."

When she came to see me in her early thirties, Jane was still struggling to find spiritual peace. Before she could put her early religious experiences into realistic perspective, she needed to reflect upon and accept her own vulnerability as a child, traumatized by religious zealots.

Jane's search for spiritual fulfillment eventually led her to an advanced degree in religious studies to explore the commonalities in religions worldwide. She refused to adopt a specific faith but identified herself as a deeply spiritual person often giving seminars on the origins of theism.

Words of comfort, skillfully administered, are the oldest therapy known to man.

—Louis Nizer

8

Perseverance and Hope

Young Sons Deal with Divorce

Zachary, age eight, and Justin, four, came to see me a few days after learning that their parents were going to divorce. I asked them each to draw what the divorce felt like to them. Justin said he couldn't draw that, so I suggested he just use some colors to tell me about his feelings. Zach drew a large red heart with a jagged crack down the middle. On each side of the heart, he drew half of a sturdy-looking brown house with equal proportions. Justin watched intently and, wanting to imitate his older brother, drew an oval shape with some squiggly lines down the middle. He told me it was a heart that had "broked places." Zach said his heart meant the "divorce was sad and he would have to live in two houses now."

I told the boys' parents that Justin would likely continue to look to his older brother Zach for help in understanding what divorce meant. Zach's picture illustrated the emotional impact of the divorce; but it also indicated understanding, acceptance and a sense of security that he would have two strong, yet separate homes now.

A few sessions later, as a way to assess their moods, I had the boys do a craft project and then tell a story about it. Zach chose to make a paper butterfly. Justin decided to make a cat from cut-outs that are glued on pre-made shapes. Perseverance and hope came alive in the form of a glue-sodden butterfly and a one-eyed cat.

Zach told a story about a butterfly that was "…first a caterpillar going into its cocoon when an eagle sees it and swoops down to eat it. The caterpillar tricks the eagle by looking like bird droppings and the eagle flies away. The caterpillar goes back into the cocoon and comes out a big beautiful butterfly." I asked what the butterfly had learned from his experience, and Zach said, "Never give up because you might become a big beautiful butterfly."

Justin's story was called "My Little Kitty Cat" and was about a cat "…just starting to eat when a big tiger came and roared at him, 'I'm going to eat you up.' The kitty cat had a wish that he would have wings and looked at his back and said, 'Meow, meow.' He had wings and flew up in the air away from the big tiger. When he got home there was a bowl of milk waiting for him." When I asked what the kitty had learned, Justin said, "If you don't have a wish, it can't come true."

Zach and Justin had a perspective on their parents' divorce that only young children could create. Justin was most worried about where he would sleep. Maybe his mom would let him sleep in her bed all the time now and that would be "super." Dad had bought him a special "car bed," and he hoped it wouldn't be too far away from his brother's room. He already knew that Dad's bedroom was upstairs in the new house. Justin and I hit on a plan for him to sleep in Mom's nightshirt when spending the night at Dad's house, and to sleep in one of Dad's t-shirts when spending the night at Mom's house. Somehow the new bedclothes made the transition easier. Justin's overnight bag went back and forth between houses and balled up inside was a transitional object of PJ attire.

Zach stressed over how to explain the situation to his friends. Other kids' parents came over and hugged him for "no reason" when he was waiting outside on the steps to be picked up from school. There was a lot of hugging of his mother, too. He wanted his friends not to ask too many questions, not be too sad for him, and to invite him over for more play dates. I told Zach he seemed to have some good ideas of how to manage this new situation. Friends needed to support one another.

When asked how things were with his dad, Justin told me he was "always walking back and forth." When asked to show me what he meant he did a good job of demonstrating agitated pacing. On the upside, his dad was playing with him more, had read him a book about divorce he got from my office, and was "doing a lot more hugging too."

Zach told me he thought there should be a law against divorce until a child was ten. He thought a person was halfway grown up at this point and didn't need two parents the way you did when you were little. He thought people should be allowed to separate because maybe they would be happier on their own, but a little kid like Justin couldn't handle it and became "a whining machine." I acknowledged that divorce could be more upsetting and confusing to younger kids, but that any child could feel disappointed and frustrated. I reminded him how much Justin looked up to him and suggested that some "big brother" talks might tone down the whining. Zach wrote down his brother's initials in a little date book I gave him and said he'd report the results to me. I later got a report from Justin that Zach had told him he would always go with him to either Mom's house or Dad's house until he was comfortable going by himself. He said this news was in Zach's special little book.

Justin invented a new way to kiss his mom goodbye. He took her to the family room and jumped up on the armrest of the couch so their height was parallel. Kissing his mom the way he had seen his daddy do it gave him a haughty satisfaction. Rubbing his forehead, he suddenly blurted out that he was going to marry her when he grew up and fell back on my couch in a blissful reverie.

Children's natural inclination is to adopt the emotions that their divorcing parents are exhibiting. Zach and Justin's parents were able to co-parent their children and agree on similar routines, responsibilities and involvement in their children's lives.

The reassurance of the love and commitment they gave to their sons helped to pave the way for the children's acceptance of the end of their parents' union, while still preserving their relationship with each parent. That children are able to take comfort in a personal fantasy, or to assert a strong opinion on how the world should really be, is one of the saving graces of youth.

Love is strongest in pursuit;
friendship in possession.

—Ralph Waldo Emerson

9

Water
Dreams

*Death of a
Childhood Friend*

There was no activity Laura enjoyed more as a child than swimming. She loved the thrill of the ocean, being carried by the waves at the mercy of the pounding surf. The sea's unpredictability was part of its appeal. Each day it offered a slightly different exhilarating experience.

She invented a solitary game of swimming out beyond the surf and diving down deep until her hands touched the ocean floor. She kept her eyes closed since it was impossible to see beneath the murky and tumultuous surface. She could feel only the currents swirling around her and swam in the direction that her senses told her was straight down.

After swimming down 10 or 12 feet, she would find the bottom and then right herself to spring off its sandy floor. Breathless, she would reach the ocean surface and its blinding sunlit waves. Laura would challenge herself not to turn for the surface until she had touched the sandy depths. The ocean became a kind of haunted abyss, where an unfamiliar sensation often gave her the impulse to flee to the surface.

Then Laura had a dream that changed her relationship with water forever. She was swimming by herself in what seemed to be a clear lake or pool with no shore. Diving down deep, she could still see the sunlight sparkle as it cut through the water. She saw herself twirling, changing directions, and swimming in movements that paralleled dancing. The water held her in tranquility and beauty until suddenly she became out of breath. Completely disoriented and frantic she swam aimlessly as her breath slipped away. Then paralyzed, she realized there was no escape. She looked down at her legs to find nothing there. She was becoming the water. Only her head and torso were left when she awoke, gasping for air.

Laura had often played Super-lady with her childhood friend Mary. She remembered how they would run in their floppy high-heels, holding hands, with their dishtowel capes flying from their necks. When they were both ten, Mary drowned in a lake while her family was having a waterside picnic. Laura's mother got the phone call while her family was vacationing at the beach. A few weeks later Laura had the dream, and her connection to water was never the same. She wondered if she could have saved Mary if she had been at the picnic that day, or if they both somehow would have drowned together. Laura was still drawn to the ocean, but its depths now held the memory of Mary.

Laura came to see me when she was an at-home mom with two preschool children. She had suffered from depression during college. For awhile her depression subsided, but then it recurred just before she started therapy with me.

She had started a summer business of teaching swimming lessons to young children, and although the business was going well, she found herself thinking often of her childhood friend Mary. Her relationship with Mary had been especially close, as deep as her feelings for her parents and siblings. She recalled the day they became "blood sisters," pricking their index fingers with a sewing needle and pressing their fingers together while pledging to be life-long friends. With foreheads touching and hands clasped, they whispered, "Till death do us part."

Laura's grief and guilt were finally resolved as a result of a new dream that came to her during the time of our summer therapy sessions.

She was standing on a hill with a small group of people after a hike, overlooking a murky lagoon. Laura watched her friend's young son, who couldn't swim, lean over and peer into the water. Suddenly, she realized he was going to fall in, and she watched his small body plummet into the swampy pond. Everyone rushed to the spot where he had disappeared. Laura thought that surely his body would rise to the surface right where he fell in. As if rooted to the ground, she and her friends stared transfixed at the water and desperately shouted his name.

When the child failed to appear, Laura knew she must attempt to rescue him. She dove in, but her cumbersome boots made it impossible to reach far enough down into the water. As she fought their buoyancy, she knew that she might fail in her attempt to save the little boy. Laura rose to the surface for a breath of air and heard the pleading voices of her friends. She tugged her boots off and dove down again, leaving the boots to bob on the surface.

Under the water, the shape of a crate dimly emerged, and Laura reached in and touched the little boy's arm. His hands were clutching the slats of the crate, and Laura firmly pried them loose. The little boy had panicked and sought safety inside the crate, but instead was drowning himself. Holding him close to her, she swam frantically to the air above.

This dream had a profound connection to reality. When Laura awoke, she recognized the boy in the dream as one of the children in her swimming classes. She had been anxious about teaching him to swim because he was a frail child who needed a feeding tube attached to his navel as a result of a congenital digestive disorder. When swimming, his feeding tube was reminiscent of an umbilical cord and made him appear like a large infant in a vast womb-like pool. Metaphorically, the pool had become a water or blood connection between Laura and the frail child.

I suggested to Laura that the dream might symbolically recall her relationship with Mary (her blood sister) and Laura's guilt at not having rescued her from a murky death. In the dream, Laura overcame the obstacles of her boots, the coffin-like crate, and the murky pool, all indications of her vulnerability in the water. I urged Laura to recognize her strong side which had persisted through fear and difficulty toward the resolution of saving the child.

Interestingly, Laura did not know in the dream if the child would recover or not. The impact of the dream was not in the final outcome, however, but in Laura's recognition of her own valor and her dedication to her childhood friend. In the dream, she had found both the courage and the competence to descend to the depths and to revive the spirits of both herself and Mary.

The greatest happiness of life is the conviction that we are loved, loved for ourselves, or rather loved in spite of ourselves.

—Victor Hugo

10

Death Anniversary

Loss of a Brother

Lucas told me his younger brother, Niko, had died of leukemia nearly a year ago. In a few months, his family would be meeting in Colorado to spread his brother's ashes in a place where the family used to vacation. Lucas had recently moved to Phoenix and had begun an internship, but he was falling into a depression. "I can't stop thinking about Niko," he lamented. He wondered why he was feeling so low, when he'd already been through the process of Niko's death and dying. Lucas could not put out of his mind the images of his 18-year-old brother's body gradually wasting away, and then finding him lying lifeless with his arm resting against his computer.

I asked him about his regrets. Lucas told me he knew he had "survivor's guilt" and feared that he had not spent enough time with his brother, particularly toward the end. I asked him to describe his day-to-day life with Niko while Lucas was still living at home. He told me his mother had cared for Niko 24 hours a day. Niko slept intermittently for most of the day, played his video games in solitude and, when inspired, made cartoon doodles of his favorite characters.

Lucas would visit his brother's room each evening after school to talk, listen to music and play video games. Niko quizzed Lucas about his life as if for vicarious engagement: which girl had currently caught his eye, in what classes he was having to pull all-nighters, and where Lucas and his friends would be hanging out. Lucas always felt guilty describing the particulars and would usually try to dismiss them as unimportant and too mundane.

Niko would become frustrated and say, "Get a grip, Luke, you have a great life."

I asked Lucas what he thought his brother might have been needing from him at the time. He told me he now knew Niko had wanted him to be happy too and to share his experiences. Lucas hadn't realized before that being with his friends, describing his new girlfriend and completing his research paper were all experiences Niko desperately wanted to hear about. "I thought I was taking something away from him when I shared my life with him, not that I was giving him something to hold onto. I couldn't understand why he was so damn happy for me all the time," he said. We eventually concluded that perhaps Niko had made peace with his death and that his final desire may have been to live through his brother until the end.

During one session, Lucas wanted me to see some valued stones he kept in a leather pouch that each held a memory of Niko. One by one, he fingered each stone and related funny and tender stories about his memories connected with it. He punctuated his reminiscences with, "I should have a been a better brother."

I told him I thought many people felt that way after a significant loss; we often judge ourselves harshly in retrospect. I asked him to appraise himself from his brother's point of view. He looked surprised and said his brother idolized him, causing Lucas to feel disingenuous. "Possibly, we evaluate our lives from our own needs and perspectives," I offered. "Maybe, during your brother's illness, you were exactly who your brother needed you to be. Can you take some pride and comfort in that?"

Lucas wept in every session. The tears Lucas shed were a steady flow, but he would simply talk through them, never skipping a breath or interrupting the cadence of his speech. It was not even apparent he was crying, unless you were looking at him and noticed his stream of grief.

Lucas's insurance company had authorized twelve sessions. The last one fell just two weeks before the anniversary of Niko's death. I gave Lucas a stone at our last meeting, a tiger's eye, to add to the collection in his leather pouch. "Your pain is only as deep as your love," I reminded him. He thanked me, shook my hand, and I watched through my window as he walked with easy strides to his car. That was the only session in which he didn't weep.

Lucas had grown up with an older brother's sense of duty to act as protector and guardian to his younger brother. He had walked his brother to school, cheered him on in sports, kept the bullies away and later drove him to Boy Scouts. When Niko got sick, it was almost as if Lucas had made an error somehow: not supervised him well enough, let him smoke an occasional cigarette, stay out too late, or committed some other transgression that had cost Niko his life. Lucas wanted to be able to place blame, even if it was on himself.

Lucas relived every minor violation of brotherly love, real or imagined, in an effort to attribute cause and effect. Lucas had played a few practical jokes on Niko that now seemed like deeds of monstrous selfishness. He had let go of the back of the bike Niko was learning to ride without training wheels while running beside him, promising at the top of his voice that he was holding on. Niko hit a bump and flew headfirst over the handle bars, cracking his head open and requiring several stitches. Niko had cried as he saw the drops of blood fall onto his shirt, but his concern was for Lucas as he apologized for "falling off." Niko died with that small scar over his left eyebrow.

Lucas also remembered Niko's first date and how he had come to Lucas to check out his clothes for the evening. Lucas had Niko change clothes several times before giving his approval with a "that's a pass." Lucas had prided himself on giving his brother a periodic "once over gaze," as if assessing Niko's appearance and stature as a young man. This nonverbal one-upsmanship usually resulted in a half-hearted punch from Niko to quit harassing him. Niko, in turn, had never second guessed Lucas about anything. Having Niko in his shadow had seemed to Lucas like his birthright, but now he felt it had been a blessing he hadn't deserved.

The hardest year was when Lucas left for his first year of graduate school, when Niko relapsed. The doctors had warned of that possibility, but no one had suggested Lucas should not go back to school. Lucas now had regrets that he had stayed in school as time had slowly slipped away for Niko. I suggested that Niko had not judged Lucas, but had given him unconditional love. He might even have felt the bike incident, first date and "once over gaze" to be humorous. If not, he surely would not have found any malicious intent in Lucas' playful mockery.

Survivor's guilt compels the survivor to magnify any behaviors or feelings which confirm wrongdoing. After revisiting a number of childhood experiences and the memories of the year prior to Niko's death, Lucas was finally able to free himself of any responsibility or blame. He had not been next to Niko's bedside like his mother had, but he had shared his life with Niko, even while in graduate school. If Lucas had put his own life on hold, there would have been no stories to tell Niko, no future plans to share and no expectations of a homecoming. There would have been no album of pictures from graduate school, no surprise gifts in the mail, and no lengthy phone calls. Niko never would have been able to say, "I heard from Lucas today." Maybe absence does make the heart grow fonder, for when Lucas returned home, Niko was able to die quietly within days of his brother's embrace.

"Great Spirit, help me never to judge another until I have walked in his moccasins."

—Sioux Indian Prayer

11

The Crush

Boundaries in
Young Love

He was 22 years old, employed by her father, and the answer to the fantasies of Dana, a ten-year-old girl. The long days of her summer were spent as his little companion at the swim club where he was the coach and lifeguard. Dana would tease him about being a "hairy ape man" pointing out the blond ringlets that covered his chest, arms and legs. He played along with this ancestral relationship to Tarzan and told her adventure stories of his life in the jungle. He would pick her up by letting her hang from his flexed arm and assure her that his strength came from swinging on the jungle vines in Africa. Play fighting, teasing, helping him with his duties and creating their fantasy life was her daily occupation. "Will you marry me when I grow up?" she'd tentatively ask and he'd reply, "Sure thing, kiddo," as he tousled her hair.

Her first experience of sexual arousal was with him, innocence betrayed by a mutual attraction. He was teaching a lifesaving class to a group of novice lifeguards, and Dana had been watching. Suddenly, he motioned for her to come over and asked her to lie down so he could demonstrate mouth-to-mouth resuscitation. He laid out the towel he had wrapped around his waist and leaned over her as she lay down. Telling her to relax and close her eyes, he cradled her head and tilted it backwards. Closing her nostrils with his hand and covering her lips with his mouth, he began to breathe gently into her.

His breath was inside of her again and again, when it occurred to her that having sex must be like this. A part of someone else filling you up so there was no separation; you just merged. When he was finished, Dana couldn't move and she recalled hearing him call her name several times as she struggled to pull herself from her reverie.

After that day, everything changed and she felt like a stranger next to him. There was no more teasing or pretending, and he would pull away when she would try to touch him. Dana decided on a final test. One morning she took a package of M&M's and spelled out his name neatly on the counter top inside his office at the club. "He loves me, he loves me not" she silently repeated to herself. "If he eats them, he loves me and if he throws them out, he loves me not," she decided.

By mid-afternoon she could wait no longer and quickly shot a glance at an empty counter and then to the nearby trash. Her heart leapt with the thought that maybe he had eaten them and everything would be all right again.

Then she saw the paper cup pushed aside on the counter, a dixie cup full of her M&M's. She hadn't planned for this response, but surmised that this was his way of saying their Tarzan play was over.

Dana had understood that a line had been crossed, but she was unsure who had crossed it. That pivotal summer their fantasy had dipped into reality and left them both shaken. Dana never ate those M&M's, but buried them in her backyard, one by one, as she said good-bye to him. Her crush had become a confusion, one that was still troubling enough to disentangle in therapy almost twenty years later.

Not every young person experiences a crush, but many do, girls and boys developing an infatuation for someone, usually a teacher, coach or mentor in their life. The word alone describes the heartbreak involved in the dissolution of a relationship that was "too soon in time." It is likely born of the adolescent's feelings of idealization and can create an attachment of such strength that its end can be a crushing blow.

For Dana it was a slow process, lasting years, to give up a fantasy that had been a huge delight to both her and "her man," as she liked to call him. During the winter they did not see one another, but when summer came they reunited at the swim club. After the lifesaving demonstration, however, they fell further and further apart. When Dana was twelve he got engaged and later married. She attended the wedding, numb with the confusion of him promising to wait for her and yet her knowing full well, at least then, the impossibility of a real future together. Why had it all been so painful for her in those early years?

Dana agreed that the rite of passage that a first love relationship brings is often painful, and that we come back to those experiences in our thoughts and feelings as we develop other love relationships. It is akin to grieving our first loss over and over with every new loss we experience. This man had been her first attachment to a male other than her father (her initial love and the man she intended, at age four, to marry). Didn't it make sense that once she outgrew that ambition she would turn to a father figure who teased her about

107

his heritage to Tarzan and even worked for her father? I offered that explanation to Dana as a point of view to consider in understanding this transitional relationship during her youth.

Yet a boundary had been crossed many years ago, both physically and emotionally, which each of them had recognized and which had resulted in bringing a natural end to their fantasy. Dana decided that neither one of them had anything to be ashamed of and that she had not been consciously taken advantage of by him. In fact, it may have frightened him far more than it had excited her.

Dana's first concern when she came to see me had actually been for her son and a kind of parallel experience she was seeing unfold. Kenneth was 11 and had a crush on his sixth grade teacher, Miss Lewis. According to Kenneth, his teacher would put her hand on his shoulder, tell jokes, call him "Kenny boy," and had worn at least a dozen pairs of stylish high heels to school. His mother thought Kenneth seemed far too attuned to Miss Lewis' habits and appearance. Feeling guilty that she may have helped fuel the flames, Dana regretfully confessed to buying some potted flowers for Kenneth to bring to school as a token of his affection.

We discussed how to normalize his strong feelings by having both parents talk about crushes with Kenneth and the boundaries that should stand between him and his teacher. I encouraged Dana to open up a dialogue with Kenneth to discover what his expectations might be in this relationship. Innocence needed to be protected and preserved, but not at the expense of condemning this relationship as inappropriate or exploitative.

Her son's disclosures gradually led Dana and her husband to the shared confidence that Miss Lewis' relationship was one of platonic and playful caring. For Kenneth, I suggested that Dana had to be cognizant of appropriate boundaries and build trust with her son, so if he needed his mother's counsel she would be there to listen and advise. I also knew that Kenneth might keep a memory of Miss Lewis, someday accompanied by a sigh and shake of his head, just as his mother remembered the imprint of her first crush.

*What doesn't kill me makes
me stronger.*

—Albert Camus

12

Violated

Recovery From Rape

The summer Jen graduated from college, she decided to move to San Francisco to begin her life as an independent adult. Within a few weeks, she had rented a flat near Market Street, gotten a job as a temp and rescued a puppy from the Pound. Then something happened that cut so deeply that she kept its reality at bay for years.

One morning, she decided to visit the aquarium at Golden Gate Park. She was outside next to the fountain, waiting for the aquarium to open when a teenager with a slight build came up to her. He described a dog he had lost and wondered if she had seen it. She hadn't, but she excitedly told him about her new Shepherd puppy that she had left at home. The boy seemed younger than Jen, and had a quiet, friendly manner about him.

With a slight shrug, he invited her to "get stoned" with him. She was reluctant, but he was gently persuasive, and soon she was following him up a hill to a secluded spot in the trees. They sat leaning against a huge pine tree while he carefully unwrapped his "stash." She thought it would be a marijuana joint, but it was a white powder instead. He ritualistically formed it into a line on a book of matches and showed her how to close one nostril and inhale it. One line for him and two for her.

Jen's next memory was of a struggle. She was on the ground and was pushing against him with all her might. His lips were aggressively pressing against her own and she was becoming out of breath. His face appeared broken, as if seen through a kaleidoscope. The distorted fragments of his facial features bore down on her.

Then she thought she felt the pine tree inside her, scraping her with rhythmic movements. It had seemed to fill up her entire body. Nothing made sense. Waves of pain and nausea swept over her until she blacked out.

Later when Jen awoke, she saw that it was sunset. She tried to stand up against the tree, but was overcome with dizziness and again lost consciousness. She remembered walking aimlessly through the moonlit park, vomiting. There seemed to be a bottomless pit of liquid inside her that needed to escape. It had a will of its own, and she was simply the vessel that responded. A couple approached Jen and asked if she needed help. Immediately relieved, she told them her address and clung to the woman's arm as they walked her to their car.

At home she vomited a few more times. While in the bathroom, she noticed dirt on the inside of her thighs and a bloodstain on her underwear. The boy's grotesque face flashed before her, and she relived the nightmare of the tree inside her. Suddenly, she knew the truth—that she had been raped by the young boy. His meek and mild facade had masked his evil act of violation. Alone on the hill, drugged to unconsciousness, Jen had been vulnerable, even to her own death. Her purse was gone and never recovered, and for years her sense of personal worth was held hostage.

Ten years after the rape, Jen came to see me on the advice of her internist, who thought she might be depressed. She was married, the mother of two children, and she had expressed vague symptoms of feeling blue, lack of energy and a sense of hopelessness. Jen felt as if she was viewing her life through a filtered lens. Although everything looked as it should, she couldn't embrace the feelings of security and joy that should have emanated from the picture before her. Everything good in her life seemed tenuous, as though it could slip away with the least provocation.

In one early session Jen confided that she didn't deserve to have her wonderful children, devoted husband and supportive extended family. She also told me about a friend of hers who had been sexually assaulted a few months earlier. Jen was distancing herself from the relationship, instead of trying to console and reach out to her friend. I asked her to tell me if there had been any event in her own life which might resemble her friend's plight. She immediately confided that she was a rape victim herself and had attempted to suppress the memory for years. I reminded her that all of our memories are stored in our unconscious mind, which is timeless, and that present events could trigger a memory that was emotionally unresolved.

Jen thought the circumstances of her rape were so bizarre that possibly it wasn't as traumatic as it would have been for someone who was conscious at the time. I suggested that her unconscious state might have been protective in some ways, but that it had left her completely vulnerable in other ways.

"I never thought about it because I was drugged at the time. It was more like a dream of being raped, but I know it really happened. I tried to tell myself it wasn't really rape. I was scared, and I just wanted to pretend it hadn't happened," she explained.

I asked Jen to talk about her feelings about herself after the rape. She disclosed that she had the classic symptoms of shame, guilt, and self-denigration. How could she have been so stupid as to let a boy, younger and smaller than her, overpower and violate her? Maybe she was being punished for something. She felt robbed, tainted, as if her innate goodness had been stolen. Jen had no sympathy for herself.

I asked her if she had ever sought therapy regarding the rape, and she recounted a visit to a psychiatric resident at U.C. San Francisco Hospital. "She had an agenda; she wanted me to cry, and she wanted it on audio-tape." Jen said the resident kept adjusting the tape recorder, saying she needed a recording for her supervisor, and then kept twisting her necklace in knots while Jen attempted to answer her questions. "She kept telling me to cry, but it was more like a command than a consolation. I was beyond crying. Crying is when you are breaking, and I was already shattered. By the end of the session, I felt I'd been almost strangled by the incessant knotting of that necklace."

I told her she was likely feeling re-victimized during that session. The therapist, perhaps ineptly, had been attempting to put her in touch with the helplessness she had felt at the time of the rape. It had probably been too soon at that time for Jen to confront her feelings of devastation. Even now, she needed help to recognize that she was both a victim and a survivor. She needed to experience compassion for herself and to rid herself of a self-imposed scarlet letter.

Jen came to see me for several months, went to support groups for rape survivors and studied the reading material I gave her. She was able to bring the shadow of her past into the light and begin to embrace her life anew. Slowly, she was able to identify with the experiences of other rape victims and relinquish her own shame and self-judgment. She allowed herself the empathy she felt for others. The fact that she had been drugged did not lessen the trauma of being violated. It had rendered her helpless to a wolf in sheep's clothing.

Nothing we ever imagine is beyond our powers, only beyond our present self-knowledge.

—Theodore Rozak

13

The Fish and The Tree

Learning Impulse Control

Eight year old Simon routinely had to use the bathroom during his therapy sessions. He wasn't unusual in that respect; many of my younger clients needed the physical or psychological relief of disrupting the sessions to use the facilities. For Simon, however, it was a test of his impulse control and the main reason his parents had sought therapy for him.

My Japanese fighting fish Blue lived in a fishbowl in the bathroom. Blue had a personality, of sorts. He came up to say "hello" if you put your fingers against the glass, I suppose, in an expectation of being fed. If you put your face against the glass to peer at him, he would inflate his gills to appear bigger than he was.

Simon was entranced.

On successive bathroom breaks, Simon reported that Blue had jumped out of his fish bowl, but that Simon had rescued him. The first time, I didn't pay much attention to what I assumed was Simon's tall tale, until I went into the bathroom after he left and found water spilled outside the fish bowl.

The next session when Simon requested to use the bathroom, I reminded him that it was dangerous for Blue to be out of the water and would Simon please check on him. Again, he reported that Blue had jumped out and that he had saved Blue in the nick of time.

I decided a confrontation with Simon would not be productive, so I suggested we measure the water level, which might be too high. I told Simon how important Blue was to me and to all my younger clients. He needed to be protected from danger. Simon said he loved Blue, too; but in the following session Blue was almost loved to death.

Simon yelled from the bathroom, "Hurry, hurry, come quick. Blue is on the floor!"

As I quickly turned into the bathroom doorway, I saw a wilted Blue lying on the floor and saw Simon scoop him up and drop him back into the fish bowl. Immediately, Blue began swimming, his fins and tail in perfect form. "I saved him! I saved Blue for you," Simon said in triumph.

I told Simon that was true, but it might not always be possible. Each time Blue was out of the water could make him weaker, and the fall itself might hurt him. I reminded Simon we would both feel badly if Blue died.

Back in the consulting room, Simon asked if I thought he dropped Blue on the floor. I told him I knew he wanted to save Blue and be a hero, but taking Blue out of the water was too dangerous. When I told him our time was over for that day, he hesitated and then said, " I dropped Blue on the floor. I'm sorry. Does that mean I'm a bad kid?"

I told him I appreciated his apology and that I thought it meant he needed to do more play in my office where he could pretend to be a hero. For months afterward, Simon pretended he was the EMT in a helicopter saving animals and people from all kinds of disasters: fires, volcanoes, tornadoes, earthquakes, avalanches and (after he read a book about natural disasters) even a tsunami.

After Blue's episode on the floor, I decided I wanted neither Simon nor I to feel the guilt associated with his demise in another out-of-bowl experience. I moved Blue out of the bathroom and into the consulting room. One day, Simon asked if he could use the fish bowl as a lake and drop an action figure into the water. I granted permission, asking him to do so very carefully. The action figure was bobbing just below the surface when Simon proceeded to call for the emergency helicopter, flying it quickly across the room. He explained that a man was drowning because his boat had hit a rock hidden under the surface of the water.

As Simon lowered the rope for the action figure to grab onto, we both noticed that Blue was actually nudging its shoulder, causing the arm to rise slightly out of the water. "Blue is helping me save him. He could eat him, but he's saving him," Simon said, excitedly.

Blue had retreated to the other side of the bowl when Simon hailed him with a "Thanks, buddy." He carried the dripping action figure across the room and spoke into his cupped hand, as if into a walkie talkie, "Rescue completed, rescue completed. Over and out."

In a session later that year, I asked Simon, "What is your favorite activity at home or your favorite way to play?"

"I don't have one," he responded, "but I do have a favorite place to be."

"Is that your room?".

"No, you would never guess it. It's in my tree," he confided. "My tree is an old pine tree that has a lot of branches inside, and you can climb up the middle and hide in the needles. I go there all the time."

I learned that Simon sat in his tree (designated "his" because he had claimed it, and no one else said otherwise) almost every day and sometimes twice a day. His mom thought he was just looking around up there, his dad thought it was exercise, but his older sister thought it was weird. It turned out to be none of the above.

I was pleasantly surprised to find out what Simon said he was really doing up there for 20 or 30 minutes, sometimes longer. He was dreaming. Simon liked to daydream, and he needed a secluded, private place to free his imagination. Some of his most memorable dreams included flying on an eagle's back through the clouds, winning a trophy for saving some dolphins, surfing the largest wave in the world, getting all "A's" in his school work, and healing his ill grandpa.

His dreams ranged from the fantastic to the mundane. Sometimes he shared that he couldn't remember the dream at all, yet he still climbed out of the tree feeling much better than when he climbed up it. I thought he must be falling asleep in the tree, but the more he talked, I decided that he had induced himself into a meditative state.

"What is the first thing you think of after you've climbed up your tree?"

"I don't think of anything. I just listen— the sound of the wind blowing through my tree is the best, but if it isn't windy I listen to the birds tweeting or to my breath coming out of my nose." Without any guidance and entirely by intuition, Simon had taught himself to meditate and achieve a sense of well-being.

His pediatrician's dire assessment, however, was that Simon was withdrawing socially or even becoming pre-psychotic. He pronounced that children do not normally sit in trees and that

Simon needed to be playing, not daydreaming. I urged his parents not to take away Simon's tree just yet because the issue deserved further evaluation.

In a group conference including Simon's parents, myself, his pediatrician, his grandparents, and his school principal, the following determinations were reached. Simon's grades had improved over this past year, he was socially appropriate at school and he had play dates regularly. He was less impulsive at home, had more control over his emotions and seemed more content in the last several months.

His grandfather spoke last, saying he thought it was "hogwash" to be so nervous about a boy climbing a tree, and so what if he did it alone, or sat there for a while. He had done the same thing when he was a kid, and they called him "son of a tree" because he often wouldn't come down. Wasn't this a better activity than watching TV, playing video games, or enacting wars with super heroes? Simon's grandpa gave us all something to think about.

We reached the conclusion that the best thing to do was simply to monitor Simon. He could climb his tree when he felt like it; people would not comment on being concerned about "his habit" and would not think of it as a negative. This was just playful daydreaming or possibly meditation, which has been deemed therapeutic for centuries. We were all to keep our guard up, however, and watch for signs that Simon's tree sitting was becoming compulsive.

Once, Simon decided to draw me his tree, using an entire sheet of paper. He used only two colors, green and brown, with the branches spread out beyond the edges of the paper. Simon drew himself leaning against a branch jutting out from the trunk, enclosed in the greenery of the needles. He wanted me to know how the tree looked from the inside.

Simon agreed to record his daydreams in a tape recorder for awhile. That was when I learned he experienced recurrent dreams. I looked for common themes. Never was there a negative image, unlike the dreams most of us have when we are asleep. They were primarily dreams of success, accomplishment, and compassion, which in themselves brought him peace. I asked him to describe to me the feeling he had when he would climb down from the tree. He told me, "I don't feel anything until I walk inside and then I just feel perfectly ok. Not happy, because I'm not excited, but I feel like I'm ready for the next thing. Kind of like, I was feeling closed when I went up the tree, and then when I climbed down I felt open."

When Simon was older, I learned that he used his tree less and less. Occasionally, however, he would climb up there particularly, his parents informed me, when there was any stress going on. At 12, he was somewhat embarrassed by his ritual, sensitive to the long debates there had been about it.

I told him I hoped he would remember that he had stumbled onto something that costs nothing, that he could perform almost anywhere in private, and that leaves him with a sense of tranquility. That the tranquility is transitory doesn't really matter, for it may later sustain him in times of stress. Simon discovered this age-old truth, on his own and before his ninth birthday, just by climbing a tree.

"Where love rules, there is no will to power; and where power predominates, there is love lacking. One is the shadow of the other."

—Carl Jung

14

Survival

*Physical Abuse
and Neglect*

Beth told me she had often done her middle school homework holding rubber-banded bags of ice chips against her face. She made the chips herself with a hammer and doubled the plastic bags to protect against the occasional tear. The ice was for the swollen lips she suffered when her mother would smack her in the face, invariably hitting her in the mouth.

I asked her about the impetus for this rage, mother against daughter. Beth assured me she did not scream at her mother, call her names, or defy her. However, Beth would stand her ground with her mother, particularly when it concerned "Daddy bashing."

"She was bitter and enraged after my father left her and would tell me horrible things about him, many that I felt were meant to be personally hurtful," Beth confided. "It was as though she got some satisfaction out of claiming he left me, too, and that we were both unloved."

Beth's mother insinuated that her father's neglect in sending child support payments was irrefutable proof of rejection. "I couldn't let myself believe her, and he often gave me a different story when I would ask him, so I became his defender," she explained.

Beth described the development of a vicious cycle of her mother's negative comments about her father, her contradiction of her mother's assessment, and her mother's eruption into a rage. "How out of control was she?" I asked.

Beth remembered being chased down the hall, being slammed into the wall and desperately shielding herself from her mother's hands. Sometimes she made it to her room and could lock the door before her mother could get to her. Other times, she was not so lucky and would have to make up stories to explain her swollen lips to her friends. The exception was her best friend, who often said, "Your mother must have been a crazy woman last night," while gently shaking her head in disbelief.

One day, Beth had actually feared for her life. That particular night she dashed for the safety of her closet, but her mother caught her and shoved her through the neatly hung clothes, slamming her head against the closet wall. Holding on to Beth's long hair with one hand over each of her ears, she pulled Beth's head violently back and forth. Beth recalled hearing the repeated thud of her head against the wall, but the worst sound was something else.

"At the time," she said, "I thought my mother sounded like a wild animal. She didn't say any words, it was just a sound, and I thought it meant she wanted to kill me."

Although very frightened by her mother's rages, Beth decided she would try to stop them. She vowed that the next time things escalated between them, she would warn her mother to stop or she would fight back. That day soon came when the two started to have words in the kitchen, but Beth didn't try to run to her room. When her mother lunged at her, Beth shouted, "If you hit me, I'll hit you back!"

Her mother slapped her hard across the face, and Beth swiftly gave her a low blow to the belly with her fist. Clutching onto the counter and taking a few steps backwards, her mother curled over and tried to catch her breath. The drama of her mother's reaction frightened and confused Beth, but she suspected it was her mother's histrionics at play.

She accepted the grounding her mother gave her for the attack, but curiously the hitting stopped. It was over. Beth then became like a shadow in her own home, her real life revolving around school, friends, and a locked door behind which she would blow cigarette smoke out her bedroom window. A year later she left home for good.

I asked her if she thought she had been abused during her adolescent years. She said she had never thought of her mother's behavior that way; it was just "hitting" or "being a mad woman."

"I didn't want to believe I had a bad mother," she said. "If I had a bad mother, then that might have meant I was a bad girl."

Beth hitchhiked to San Francisco when she was 16, quickly hooking up with another runaway who was only 14. Brad and his dog Bosco had walked up behind her when she had heard, "Hey good-lookin, can you spare a dime?" They struck up a friendship that lasted almost a year, living on the streets, sleeping under picnic benches and in alleys behind trash bins or on the streetcars. Panhandling was lucrative on some days, enough to buy good food, stay overnight in a motel or catch a movie. Everyone thought they were a couple since Brad was slightly taller than Beth, yet if anything she was like a big sister, prodding him to get up, clean up, and make a day's living.

The day Bosco was hit and killed by a car was a turning point for Brad. He became withdrawn and childlike, didn't wash or comb his hair for weeks. Beth was undone. She babied him, cajoled him, implored him and ignored him, but nothing brought Brad's spirit back. On impulse, Beth went to the animal shelter one day and brought home a puppy for Brad, a scruffy, skinny pup that the shelter said was refusing to eat. Beth told them she had an aunt who would take care of it. They didn't charge her, assured her the pup was otherwise healthy and supplied her with a box carrier and small blanket.

Brad was sleeping when Beth awoke him by putting the puppy into his arms. He didn't speak for the longest time or really even look at Beth. He just held that puppy and quietly cried. So little love in his life that a puppy could fill the emptiness, she thought.

Brad's energy came back almost simultaneously with the gift of Bruno. He got even more money from the tourists around Fishermen's Wharf, guessing rightly that they would rather feed a puppy than a hungry, lonesome teenager.

Brad shared the money with Beth and told her every day that she had saved his life. "You save yourself when you save someone else," she thought each time he bumped her shoulder and whispered, "If not for you…"

Near Christmas time, they decided to part since the weather was continuously damp and cold. Beth was looking for a job, and Brad had saved enough money for a bus ticket to Arizona, where he had an uncle and had heard the sun always shines. As a farewell gift, Beth bought him a pair of sunglasses and a new collar for Bruno.

Soon after Brad left, Beth got a job as a Nanny for the McWhirters, a family of Irish

Catholics with three young children, all round and rambunctious. She learned to boil cabbage, potatoes and meat, which simmered for hours in one big pot. In the evening they all sat around a table together, and when the others were finished she would feed the baby and clean up the dishes.

She left at eight o'clock after reading stories and tucking in the children, who affectionately called her Nanny Bethie. Usually, Beth slept in a nearby park with various other homeless people who generally looked out for one another by keeping watch for the police and sharing their penniless wealth. Beth relied on the sound of traffic, a light breeze and the glint of sunrise through the trees to wake her each morning.

On her birthday, the McWhirter family gave her a treasure box of carved cherry wood, inlaid with a beautiful design and some colored stones. Inside were pictures of the children, drawings they had made and a thank-you card addressed to "Dear Nanny Bethie." The gift brought Beth to a crossroads.

The treasure box barely fit into her backpack, so she pulled out her blankets and stuffed them under a park bench for another lost soul to shield himself from the cold. She couldn't go back to the McWhirters and tell them she had no place to keep the treasure box, nor could she give up the gift.

She decided it was time to leave, and that she could no longer carry on the charade of a high school girl living with her family and working for the pleasure of it. Taking the children to the park to play, when it was her haven at night, seemed like keeping a dark secret. She worried that one of her street friends would come over to share their picnic, or worse that old Tiger Sam, with his toothless grin, would stagger up to her and scare the children.

She wrote the family a note, thanking them for everything, and explaining her family's sudden move to Arizona. She wouldn't be coming over again but wished them well, always. Her tears smudging the ink, she folded her note and left it in their mailbox under a small blue stone.

Beth rode the bus to Phoenix. After a few weeks she got a job at a Mexican restaurant and became roommates with two of the other waitresses. She thought about Brad and if he'd actually made it to Arizona, found his uncle, and whether Bruno was still around. She remembered Brad's last name was Townsend, so she found a phone book and began calling all the Townsends in the book.

Finally, she reached Brad's uncle. Stunned, she learned that Brad had died of a drug overdose only a week earlier. There would be a funeral if she wanted to attend. The uncle complained that Bruno was always underfoot and she was welcome to take the dog off his hands.

Beth's roommate drove her to the uncle's home, a nice place in the suburbs. As the door opened, Bruno sprang into her arms. Extending a small box of Brad's belongings, his uncle said, "Brad said he had a girlfriend and I guess you must be her." Beth silently nodded, as she accepted the cardboard box and a leash for Bruno.

Sitting on her bed at home, she carefully opened the box and found everything that she had ever given to Brad: a bandana, an ID bracelet, Bosco's old collar, a picture of Beth, matchboxes, candles, movie stubs, and a pair of sunglasses.

A few weeks later, Beth called me after getting a referral from a friend at the restaurant where she worked. She was looking for a therapist to help her recover from a recent death. I asked her who she had lost and she told me, "I didn't know it then, but he was my boyfriend. I loved him."

While in therapy, Beth was able to recognize the resiliency she had shown in the face of the emotional abuse by her mother. She had fled for her own safety and had found solace and strength in working for the McWhirters. Her damaged self-image had been healed by her inclusion into the intimacy of their family. The love between Beth and Brad had been forged on a meager existence sustained by their hopes and dreams. Beth had been tenacious in rebuilding her own life, and had no way of knowing Brad was sacrificing his to drugs. She would have come to him sooner if she had known.

In a man whose childhood has known caresses and kindness, there is always a fiber of memory that can be touched to gentle issues.

—George Eliot

15

The Assassination Dream

Caring for a Dying Father

The Untouchables was a TV program based on the life of racketeer Al Capone and his nemesis, Detective Elliot Ness. Abby didn't remember the storylines, but she retained a vivid image of her father waving her away as he watched, transfixed, amid the continuous onslaught of machine gun fire. He had wanted to shield her innocent eyes from such brutality.

One night, scenes from *The Untouchables* found their way into her dream world. She could imagine no greater betrayal than the one she experienced in this dream. Abby found herself standing in her backyard next to the pole holding the clothesline, facing the alley in the twilight. She startled as a 1930's convertible screeched to a halt in front of her, carrying a firing squad of mobsters with wide-brimmed hats, trench coats and machine guns. Standing in the car, they emptied a round of ammunition toward her. Abby's clothes were shredded, and the bullets left holes in her body through which light passed. She clung to the pole of the clothesline as she felt her life draining away. There was no blood, only the feeling of slow suffocation as she tried to breathe.

As the car sped away, two men in trench coats remained talking in the dim light of the alley. Their low voices were inaudible, and she was unable to distinguish their faces until one bent down to light a cigarette. In the glow of the lighter, his profile became visible. It was her father, and with her dying breath came the realization that he had become her executioner.

This dream came to Abby shortly after her family had come home from a vacation. Her father had returned a few days earlier than the rest of the family, moved out without notice, and told his children only after they arrived, "I'm getting a divorce." Decades later, Abby was tearful as she recounted the dream, which had signified the trauma of her parents' divorce. Her unconscious had been the receptacle for the betrayal Abby felt when her father left the family.

Abby came to see me when her father was dying of lung cancer. She had quit her job to take care of him, and she was having trouble letting Hospice take over his care. His prognosis of three months to live had gradually turned into six months. Abby explained that if he died after she let Hospice take control, she would feel she had quickened his death. Yet she also wished, at times, that death would hasten her father's relief.

There was little left of the father she had known; yet even the shell of his body reminded her of many warm memories. Despite the divorce, he had been a good dad, much like a child himself, taking risks, being goofy, and never at a loss for something to do at the spur of the moment.

I told her at our first meeting that when faced with the death of a loved one, a person often reverts to the childish belief that death can be controlled. In reality, there is no justice in death, and no escape. Possibly her father would decide on his own to just let go. Abby wanted him to have a good death and for herself to come to terms with having him leave her.

They hadn't always been close. The pain of her parents' divorce, as reflected in the dream, had initially left Abby feeling rejected and betrayed. If her father loved her, why hadn't he taken her with him or sent for her to come live with him? After the divorce, he had moved to San Diego, bought a sailboat and lived on it. She wrote him long letters asking him to let her come live with him, vowing she would take care of him, cooking and cleaning so "he wouldn't have to lift a finger." He had plenty of girlfriends along the way; but he did not remarry. He would carve out several weeks each summer to be with Abby, and during those weeks the emptiness in her heart was not so deep.

Sailing on his boat with him was effortless, like flying, with the mist of saltwater on her face. For hours they would sail, with no need for conversation. Perched on the bow, she would scan the open sea and listen for her father's commands. Working in tandem, they guided "Star Bright," the sailboat he had named in honor of his daughter.

He didn't smoke when he sailed, one of the few activities he engaged in that did not invite a smoke. Otherwise, he inevitably had a cigarette in his mouth, first thing in the morning, after every meal, talking on the phone, relaxing with the TV or stereo on. In times of stress she'd hear, "I need a smoke," as he rummaged around for a lighter. The cigarettes were always available in the breast pocket of his shirt or on the night stand. Occasionally, he let Abby light one of his cigarettes, a romantic gesture she had seen on TV and in the movies. It never occurred to her that this fond memory would also be associated with his death sentence.

There came a time when there was little left to share but the rhythm of their breaths as she sat next to the bed lightly touching his hand. During that period, she rarely left his side except for visits to see me. In the quiet of the bedroom and with the gentle concentration of their breaths, she began to recall her childhood and later relayed her memories in our sessions.

Pulling her knees up to her chest, and turning slightly toward a window in my office, she looked out as if seeing her past replayed. In her earliest memory, she was just a young toddler, her dad holding her ankles as she straddled the back of his neck and rode on his shoulders. She steered him with her hands pressed against his temples. Around the house they would go until she would steer him into the wall, and there they would remain with his forehead touching the wall and him still pacing, even stepping up the pace as if he expected to go right through that wall. She would laugh so hard she would let go of his head and waver unsteadily until she felt his sure grip on her ankles.

He loved to read her story books and would change his voice to assume the identities of the characters. Sometimes he would act out the scenes, using whatever convenient props he could find in the living room. For Little Red Riding Hood, a bandana turned him into a little girl going to Grandma's through the woods; under a blanket, he became the grandma; and for the wolf, he simply rolled up the sleeves of his T-shirt, messed up his hair to create a scruffy look, baring his teeth. Abby would sit mesmerized with her arms around her knees, sometimes burying her face in them when the wolf emerged.

In middle school, she remembered games of hide and seek, kick the can and board games that lasted for hours. He loved competition, but if she begged a little, he would spontaneously change the rules so Abby could win. After he left her mother, he sent Abby books, novels, political treatises, poetry, newspaper and magazine articles that intrigued him, and wrote comments in the margin or asked her questions about them. She loved this way of relating with him, because she knew he valued her and took pride in helping her grow.

Occasionally they had disagreements, but he always let her know he respected the fact that she had opinions that might differ from his. Then he would pepper her with evidence that might convince her to come over to his side of the issue. He often convinced her, more because of the delight he showed in persuading her, than as a result of the experts he quoted.

As he was dying, she retrieved some of his letters, articles and poetry books, with asterisks proclaiming his "best selections," and began creating a scrapbook. In one envelope she found holiday and birthday cards from him that she had saved. He hadn't just signed them, but always added a special touch, changing the wording, adding a rhyme or just writing his own personal message. Those simple cards now were the touchstones of her childhood.

One day our session was devoted to whether she should tell her dad that he could let go now, that she would be all right, that he had fought the good fight and now could find deliverance in what lay beyond. He had told her one evening, between labored breaths, that he wondered if he would go back to where he was before he was born. He wanted to be released from the cancer which had sucked the life from him. He was ready.

I decided to tell Abby not to convey anything verbally, but to meditate on her thoughts while she was with him. Three days after that session, Abby called to tell me he had passed away. I asked how it had happened.

"In the evening he opened his eyes and said, 'I'm leaving soon. I'll be in the morning breeze. Go outside then.'" She continued, "The next morning I went to check on Dad, and his arm was stretched out over the side of the bed, relaxed with an open palm. He wasn't breathing and was cool to the touch. I went outside and, I'm embarrassed to say, I felt a breeze and sat down on the doorstep, saying goodbye to Dad."

Freedom is moving easy in harness.

—Robert Frost

16

Twists of Fate

*A Young Boy's Life
in a Wheelchair*

Jacob raced down my brick walkway in his wheelchair and popped a wheelie at the door to my office. "That was really impressive," I noted, as I slid open the glass door for him. He rolled in and with one huge swing of his arms, flung himself out of his chair and landed squarely on my couch.

I found myself staring at his body. His upper torso was perfectly formed down to his waist. He was almost stunning in his youthful good looks: wide smile, unruly hair, dark eyes with heavy lashes, and arms with definition I'd never seen on a 12-year-old. With averted eyes, I tried to take in his wasted legs. The size of a toddler's, they twisted to the side, like the limbs of a mangled doll. The juxtaposition of such beauty and deformity was mind-wrenching.

"Let me show you what I can do," he said as he lowered himself onto the floor with his long arms balanced on his knuckles. He quickly moved around the office, landing on furniture, standing on his hands, and doing one-arm push-ups.

"You are amazing," I said.

After a few moments, he said, "That's it, that's all I can do. God made a mistake when he made me."

I asked what made him think he was a mistake.

"Well, there are mistakes, you know, rapists, murderers, thieves."

I countered that some people believe in free will and that people had choices to behave in certain ways.

"I would never choose this," he said. "I'd rather be dead."

We talked about his recent depression and about the time he had gotten a knife out and threatened to slit his throat. He assured me he wouldn't really have done it, but he also hated his life. "I don't think I can be good at anything, at least anything I want to be good at."

"I don't think you are a mistake, so let's think of what you can do right now to feel worthwhile," I offered. "Maybe you can let others see your strength and bravery. We only know our own strength when we feel our weakness and can rise above it. One does not exist without the other."

He doubted he could feel that way, until I pointed out he was doing it at the moment. "You came in showing me how strong you are, that there are many things you can do, and you looked proud. You made me feel your strength and bravery in spite of your chair."

Two years later, I attended Jacob's eighth grade graduation. When he rolled up onto the stage he spun quickly front and center, raised his arm, pushed back the sleeve of his gown and flexed his muscle. "That was really impressive," I noted, and smiled to myself that I had revisited my first impression.

At age 16, Jacob had one ambition, and that was to kiss a girl. He said it had to be a real kiss, not something orchestrated by spin the bottle or arranged by his friends. It needed to be a girl who he liked and who liked him, in spite of his handicap. "I know it's a tall order, but it would just be so great if she was beautiful too."

"There is nothing wrong with fantasy," I told him, "and many real successes start with fantasy. Cultivate your female friendships and see what happens."

Jacob bought a mini-sculpture of the "The Kiss," by Rodin, and kept it on a shelf in his room. Three years passed before he met Mia.

"We met in the library, and it was like in the movies when the girl drops her books and the boy scrambles to retrieve them. I had to flip my wheelchair onto the back wheels and reach one arm down to scoop up her books. She looked really startled and tried to push my chair down while I was holding the books out to her. She said she thought I was going to fall.

"I told her that I never fall. Then I asked her about her chemistry class because I noticed she had the same textbook as I did." Jacob told me not only was she sweet and smart, but she was also beautiful. "If I could have made her up, Mia is who I would have created."

After three months of meeting in the library and a few coffee dates, Jacob had taken a deep emotional turn. "I've fallen in love," he told me during one session, "and I know it won't last."

"It won't last because you are only 19 years old, not because of some deficiency of yours or Mia's," I said.

It was around this time that Jacob decided that his salvation would be in a kiss from Mia. He told me that he thought he could let her go if only he could first have a kiss. I urged him to be honest about his feelings, but to be prepared for rejection. Even if she valued him as a friend, kissing might be crossing a boundary she was not comfortable with.

She invited him to visit her at her house off campus. He first had to negotiate the porch, swinging out of his chair, sitting, and then lifting himself around to get up the few steps. He was speedy and agile, even though he knew it looked awkward. He sprang off his knuckles and landed on the sofa with cushions all around him. Mia sat next to him and told him how she felt about him. "'You mean a lot to me as a friend. I do care for you. I want to give you something you can carry in your heart forever.'" As fate would have it, Mia was the instigator of the kiss, and that made it all that much sweeter for Jacob. He wanted that kiss to last for the rest of his life. He was lost in it. When Mia gently pushed him away, they both laughed. Then she got up to get them some cokes. The kiss was never repeated or ever mentioned.

I told Jacob I thought Mia had sealed their friendship with that kiss and that he would always have that memory of basking in the light of a loving girl. For a time, that experience kept him undaunted by his physical limitations. Then Jacob's family moved; he went to Europe for an operation, and I lost track of him. The memory of his struggle to find his first kiss remains compelling.

If you bring forth what is within you, it will heal you. And if you do not bring forth what is within you, it will destroy you.

—Gospel of St. Thomas

17

Dreams in Succession

Revelations From Dreams

In Juliette's first dream, she was in a session with me and suddenly was overcome by a wave of nausea. She managed only a few steps toward the office door when vomit began to spew from her mouth and onto the carpet. Worrying about the mess she was making on the floor, she started to apologize as more vomit was propelled from her mouth. She said I had run to get a bowl and was standing next to her, holding out the bowl and a small towel. I asked her if she was all right and told her she should sit back down for a minute. She then awoke with that familiar feeling of relief and exhaustion one has when a stomach virus has finally passed.

In the second dream, she found herself in a sterile hospital room with a cold tile-floor, white walls and austere furnishings, ranting and pacing back and forth across the room. Anger welled up inside her as her words ran together and expressed only a rhythm instead of coherent thoughts. I was walking behind her, dressed in a long white doctor's coat, interjecting comments of "You feel…," whenever there was a pause in her tirade. This interchange was like a synchronized rhythm, as was the pace of my steps behind Juliette while I talked over her shoulder. When she awoke from this dream, she was struck by how similar her ranting and her body language had been to Barbra Streisand's in the movie *Nuts*, which she had seen only a few days earlier.

In the final dream, Juliette anxiously ran up and down staircases in a deserted high rise building, looking for her husband. She was carrying two clear light bulbs, the shape and size of Christmas tree lights. As she looked down at them while running through a hallway, she tripped. The glass shattered and flew into her mouth. With a mouth full of glass, she carefully and painfully began to remove it, piece by piece. Juliette continued to run, frantically searching for the staircase out of the building. She was conscious of trying not to swallow or apply any pressure to the inside of her mouth, for fear of cutting herself. Methodically, she removed each shard of glass until she reached the door that led outside. It was dusk when she saw her husband standing at the end of the walkway leading up to the high rise. She was relieved he had stayed and waited for her. Juliette held out her hand, revealing the last pieces of glass, and said, "My mouth was full of glass, and these are the last two pieces."

She woke up that morning to the sunlight streaming through an open shutter.

Juliette couldn't wait to tell me about her night of three dreams and had scheduled a double session to do so. She felt there was some continuity to the dreams and wanted to discover their significance. We had analyzed her dreams before. Our explorations were usually a collaboration which led to an increased understanding of her mental illness. She had suffered from depression since her college days and had taken antidepressants for years. Now a young mother, with a husband and two small children, she had been seeing me for regular therapy for nearly a year.

These three dreams came on the brink of her family's move to Europe. I told her I thought they were historical in nature and illustrated her psychological growth. The first dream was the most primitive, with her mental illness symbolized by vomiting which she couldn't control. In that dream, she needed my compassionate side (bringing her the bowl and towel) as well as my professional interpretations. Her apologetic behavior in the dream demonstrated her early feelings of embarrassment, self-consciousness and dependence.

In the second dream, I thought she was demonstrating fear of her own anger and needed my support to express it. She still feared losing control and "being crazy." Our synchronized movements represented her sense of being validated and feeling understood by me.

In the third dream, the glass in her mouth had become symbolic of her emotional pain. I was not present, yet she was learning to confront her pain alone, "piece by piece." I explained that Freud often said that dreams of staircases represent the unconscious mind's need for expression in conscious life. The dream expressed Juliette's hope that her husband would wait for her until she was well, when she could proudly show him that her pain had been resolved.

The common thread of the three dreams was that they were all focused on Juliette's mouth. Her mouth was the vehicle for her "talk therapy" with me, where she re-experienced and resolved hurtful events from her past. Each dream had moved in the direction of growth and resolution of her inner turmoil, from the non-verbal and primitive, to verbal interchange, and then to the metaphorical.

I viewed the night of three dreams in succession as Juliette's graduation from therapy. Through a bit of serendipity, her dreams came to her just before her family's move to London, where she now resides and in her letters says she is doing well.

*Stand through life firm
as a rock in the sea,
undisturbed and
unmoved by its
ever-rising waves.*

—Hazrat Inayat Khan

18

The
Sentinel

*Turning Tragedy
into Activism*

Sam's mother became terminally ill when he was nine years old. He began therapy with the full knowledge of his mother's impending death. The doctors had urged both parents to be honest with Sam and not to build false hope. During the ensuing months, they tried to prepare Sam for one of the most profound losses a child can endure.

Sam asked all the hard questions for which I had no easy answers. When it came to matters of faith, I encouraged him to talk to his dad or asked him what he had learned in Sunday school. He would often say, "No one knows for sure," and I would agree. Uncertainty and death are intertwined. The when, where, how—and especially the why—of death, are beyond us. The foundation for faith was elusive. I commented to Sam that "faith means to believe without knowing for sure."

Sam wondered why his mom was dying and not someone else's. Was it his fault, maybe a result of the time he ate too many cookies and then denied it, or of having to be reprimanded for not listening when he knew he should? His guilt slowly dissipated, but Sam continued to be dissatisfied with the feeble answers adults have for grieving children.

I once told Sam that his memories of his mother would be like armor protecting the wound of her loss. He liked that, and it helped open the door to his reminiscences. He would often make crafts for her, recall their times together and describe his favorite things about her.

Near the time of her death, I suggested that he draw her something she would like to look at to make her feel better and show her how much he loved her. Very intently, he drew a video game warrior, complete with armor, astride a horse at the top of a mountain to the side of the sheet of paper. He drew an arrow above the figure and wrote "me" over it.

I was a little distressed that he was drawing a kind of super hero, when I'd asked that he be thinking of his mother as he drew. I kept my thoughts to myself, however, mostly because I wasn't sure how to redirect him without hurting his feelings. My fortuitous patience was rewarded. Sam turned his attention to the central part of his picture, which became a landscape of smaller mountains, a river, and a sunrise. There was subtle shading in one portion of the picture which gave it both a visual and an emotional depth.

When he finished, I asked him if his picture had a title. With his head down and after thinking a moment, he said "The Sun Rising Over a Shadow in the Valley." A revealing and healing metaphor lay before us as he carefully wrote his title in block letters, and "by Sam" in the bottom right-hand corner.

Three years later Sam's life fell into another deep abyss from which we struggled to find a way for him to emerge. Again, it was Sam who found his own way and astounded us all.

The phone call came in the middle of the night on my pager near my night table. "This is Sam's dad. I'm sorry to be calling you, but this is an emergency. I don't know what to do. How could this have happened?" his words ran together. In my sleepy state it was only at the end that I recognized who was leaving the message and called him back. My memories of Sam came flooding back. Through starts and stops, and with the same intense emotion I remembered when his wife was dying, Sam's father told me what had happened.

Sam's best friend Marcus had been killed after being hit by a drunk driver as he rode home on his bike from the grocery store. It occurred at sundown. The driver had been speeding and didn't see Marcus when his bike had veered out from around the street corner. The doctors and nurses valiantly tried to save him, but Marcus was pronounced brain dead at the hospital. His parents were calling their family and friends with the devastating news. Sam's dad wanted to wait until the morning to tell Sam, but I persuaded him otherwise.

We reached agreement that the weight of this tragedy should be shared in the moment of its impact. To deny Sam that reality might later cause him to feel guilt that he had slept as his friend had died and his family grieved. Sam would know that his father believed that he had enough strength to survive the loss of his friend. He would thereafter be able to trust that his father would always tell him the truth, even if it was crushing.

Sam's father woke him as soon as we finished talking and told him as I had suggested, "Sam, you need to wake up, something has happened. You need to know right away." Sam sensed instantly that his father was upset. A barrage of questions spilled from Sam's mouth as he clung to his father's arm and followed him into the kitchen and finally almost in a whisper said, "Tell me, tell me. I want to know." His dad told him that Marcus had been hit by a car riding his bike home from the store and he was in the hospital. His parents were at the hospital and had just called.

"My best friend is dead, isn't he?" Sam questioned. "Are they sure? Did they do everything possible? I have to see him. I have to know for myself."

Sam's dad took him to the hospital that night, and the nursing staff let Sam come into the room where Marcus lay. He thought Marcus looked like he was sleeping, no tubes, no visible trauma to his body; but his neck had been broken when his head had hit the pavement. Sam's dad had to carry his son out of the hospital room when Sam said he couldn't walk away from his friend.

At my recommendation, Sam missed school for several weeks. Most trauma experts feel a child should return to their normal routine as soon as possible after a tragic event or loss. But I felt differently about Sam and decided to respect his assertion that, for the time being, he couldn't go back to school without Marcus.

We spent a long time preparing for Marcus' memorial service, putting together pictures of him and the baseball team, gathering sympathy cards and notes from the team and other friends to make a tribute poster. "Think of something really special you could display that would show how much you loved Marcus," I suggested to Sam. He borrowed Marcus' baseball team shirt and catcher's mitt (which were later given to him by Marcus' parents) positioning them on a table at the service with his own shirt and glove. He arranged the gloves so that they lay inside one another. Beside them he placed a photograph of the two of them and wrote in the corner, "We were best friends."

Most of our sessions were devoted to putting together a scrapbook of their friendship. I encouraged Sam to write something under each photograph, memento, or drawing he included, in an effort to lock in Marcus' memory. It was to become his new set of armor.

Sam's entries included:
"We made ourselves blood brothers,
my grandpa showed me how to do it
with a pocket knife;
It was the best sleep over ever;
We agreed on everything, favorite
show, food, animal, video game, you
name it, we were in synch;
I wanted you to be my best man,
even though we were just starting to
like girls;
I'll see you again on the other side."

After several weeks, Sam turned from being sad to being angry. He was at a loss for ways to deal with his feelings. "I feel like I'm tied up with a rope, and I can't move or breathe, and I can't cut myself loose."

With careful words I addressed his dilemma, "I think you are full of rage and it feels like it's trapped inside of you with no way out. You have a right to feel angry, that's part of grieving over someone you loved. There is probably nothing in life harder to do than this."

Sam tried to take heart, but it was beyond him. "I don't care anymore, life is too unfair and nothing makes sense anymore," he lamented. He lay down and rolled over on my office couch, so he wouldn't have to look at me.

Measuring my words, I said, "Every life has a purpose, finding yours is your challenge. You will know it when it comes to you."

His anger led me to recall the organization called MADD (Mothers Against Drunk Drivers), and I told him how it was devoted to spreading the word about drunk driving and its often catastrophic consequences. Sam slowly sat up and began to listen intently. I showed him some information about MADD on the internet, in an effort to reassure him there were hundreds of thousands of adults trying to fight against the tragic events spawned by drunk driving. He left with what seemed like a more hopeful demeanor.

As it turned out, the information about MADD, which I thought might merely be comforting to Sam, spurred him into action.

During the next year, Sam became a well informed advocate and spoke at MADD events throughout the state. Its members adored Sam and found him to be poised, articulate, heartfelt and committed to the cause. Sam finished the year with periodic meetings with me and fundraisers for MADD, even ones which required that he miss school. He told me he was starting to feel free.

Out of the blue, many years later, I received a card from Sam, postmarked from his college. He remembered me, was studying architecture, had a serious girlfriend, and was in the process of organizing a campus fundraiser for MADD, where he would be the guest speaker. He wrote that, ten years later, he still keeps a picture of Marcus, in his baseball uniform, tucked away in his wallet.

ACKNOWLEDGEMENTS

I am especially indebted to my husband, David, who spent many long evenings listening, advising and editing my manuscript.

I want to acknowledge my family members and personal friends whose support and encouragement was critical to the fruition of this book. A special thanks to my teachers who taught me well and to my clients who shared the intimacy of their lives.

I deeply appreciate the work of AppleStar Publishing and my publisher, Amy Landa, whose expertise, creativity, humor and enthusiasm helped me see the light at the end of the tunnel.